LONDON CRAFT GUIDE

YARN IN THE CITY

Welcome!

This book is a natural extension of the work we've done with The Great London Yarn Crawl. When we set out to start the Yarn Crawl, our goals were to celebrate the vibrant knitting scene in London and to build a community amongst the fantastic shops and knitters here in the city.

Since we started Yarn in the City, it seems like we're constantly discovering new shops or hearing about someone with plans for one. We firmly believe that this resurgence in, and appreciation for, craft and all things handmade is only a good thing. There is growing evidence that doing things with your hands is good for you, whether it calms your mind, relieves stress or fuels your creativity. And with the burgeoning growth of online crafting communities like Ravelry and MySewingCircle, expanded resources and experts are more accessible than ever.

With the London Craft Guide we've tried to create more than a regular guide book. Profiles include information on the shops and their wares, as well as local tips on the area where the shops are located. We've also included a few holiday-friendly projects should you be overcome with creativity while inhaling the yarn- and fabric-fumes of these fabulous shops!

This is the perfect point for our disclaimer that this book is heavily skewed to a yarn and knitting point of view. After all, this is the world that we spend most of our time in, and know the best, so it's important that we make that distinction right up front. But being multi-craftual ourselves, and knowing that so many of you are as well, finding a way to include other crafts, just made sense. So we've reached out to our friends, guilds, networks, and the shops themselves for insight and recommendations on what else should be included.

The book is split into three main sections: Yarn, Fabric, and Haberdashery - just to keep things simple. In trying to organise the shop profiles in a tidy way, we found that there are those shops that could be placed in more than one of the categories. In those cases, we've slotted them in where we think they best fit, and have cross-referenced them as appropriate. One of these is The Village Haberdashery – a wonderful shop that has been part of the Yarn Crawl since the beginning. We've included it in the Fabric section because their fabric selection outnumbers their yarn options by a significant margin. Likewise for Liberty of London - even though they have the full range of Rowan yarns on offer, their prints and fabric are iconic, and are a major part of what makes Liberty so special for crafters; they couldn't have been placed anywhere else in the book.

The rest of the book includes options for daytrips with crafty highlights, as well as notes and resources to help you plan your outing. No matter if you're a new or returning visitor to London, or a local looking to explore a neighborhood other than your own, or someone trying to organise your own mini-yarn crawl with friends, we hope this book will help you.

Thank you so much for your support of Yarn in the City and making the Great London Yarn Crawl a terrific success. We would never have dared to branch out if not for your kindness and enthusiasm. Enjoy – we' ll see you in September at the next GLYC!

Best,

Allison & Rachel

Contents

HABERDASHERY

DAY TRIPS

PROJECTS

RESOURCES

YARN

Harkening back to a time when knitting yarns found in the UK were exclusively wool, many shops are still called 'wool shops' instead of yarn shops. The history of Britain is also strongly linked to the wool industry, contributing a cultural tendency amongst some (although in our experience this is largely generational) to refer to all yarns as wool, regardless of their fibre content.

Perhaps because of this British pride in its national woolly resource and history, you'll find most shops in London will have some specifically British wool available. The most common British wool in our experience is Bluefaced Leicester (or BFL), a breed of sheep originating in the UK, producing wool that is soft and lustrous. If you're looking for a properly British yarn as a souvenir in your travels, you won't go wrong with a skein of BFL.

Wool aside, the yarn shops in London will have plenty to tempt you! Most of the shops in London seem to have carved out their own niche and speciality. So while there is the inevitable overlap of some brands, in most cases each shop has something unique that you won't see anywhere else.

We've grouped our shop profiles into broad geographic categories, but don't let those designations deter you. Many of the shops are located close to each other, although they may be listed under two separate geographical sections. Our recommendation for yarn shop exploring is to pick a handful and plot a route, or you can simply stick to a given area if you're short on time. We also recommend that you check out a shop's website before you visit to make sure that opening times are up to date, or to see if there are any special events happening that you might want to join.

LOCAL TIP

I Knit has also hosted larger-scale yarn-y events in the past – such as the I Knit Fandango. If you're visiting in the spring, check out the shop's events page to see what's happening. And if you visit the shop around lunchtime, don't miss out on the street food vendors along Lower Marsh – particularly the Pad Thai!

I KNIT LONDON

106 Lower Marsh, Waterloo London SE1 7AB

I Knit bills itself as a "club, shop and sanctuary for knitters". Nestled in the heart of central London, a mere stone's throw from Waterloo Station.

I Knit stocks a wide range of gorgeous yarns from well-known commercial sources, such as West Yorkshire Spinners, Wensleydale Longwool Sheepshop, Navia, Rooster and Debbie Bliss. They also are the sole purveyors of the I Knit or Dye line, dyed in the basement of the shop. The I Knit or Dye colours can be found on fingering and laceweight yarns in a variety of fibre bases.

In addition to yarns, I Knit has a wide selection of books and patterns, needles and notions, and they have a number of social knitting events to take advantage of their on-site bar! The I Knit knitting group meets every Wednesday and Thursday nights - check the website for specific dates and times for meetups.

On the class front, I Knit offers beginner classes in knit and crochet, as well as an intermediate knitting class. They also host book launches and talks from well known industry folks, so keep an eye on their website for the latest announcements.

Also in the central area are John Lewis Oxford Street and Liberty, which we've profiled in the Fabric section, but both of which stock knitting wool, notions and patterns. ■

Contact:
iknit.org.uk
shop@iknit.org.uk
020 7261 1338

Opening hours:
Monday: 10:30am - 6pm
Tuesday - Thursday: 10:30am - 8:30pm
Friday - Saturday: 10:30am - 6pm

PATRICIA ROBERTS

60 Kinnerton Street
London SW1X 8ES

Tucked away in Knightsbridge close to fashionable Harvey Nichols and Harrods is the shop of British handknit designer Patricia Roberts.

The shop only sells her yarn, and mostly in finer gauges such as DK and 4-ply, but carries lambswool, cashmere spun in Scotland, cotton and angora yarns. You can purchase handknit women's and children's sweaters here too.

Stepping into the shop is almost like stepping back in time to when knitting was a common past time in the UK and yarn weights weren't as varied. Expect to have to wait for an answer about yardage on the yarns (they do have the information written down!), as they still do things in the traditional way by weight. The yarns come in 50 g balls (except cashmere which comes in 25 g balls), so for an average sized women's sweater you would likely need about 500 - 600 g of yarn (or 10 - 12 balls).

If you're exploring Knightsbridge and looking to get off the busy high street, Patricia Roberts is a charming shop to come and explore while you catch your breath.

Contact:
patriciaroberts.co.uk
shop@patriciaroberts.co.uk
020 7235 4742

Opening hours:
Tuesday - Friday: 10am - 6pm
Saturday: 11:30am - 6pm

LOCAL TIP

Visiting the shop is also a great excuse to wander through some of the side streets and mews in the Knightsbridge neighbourhood, which butts up against Belgravia, the former and current home of many international embassies. The shops tend to be pricey and designer, but Kinnerton Street is also home to a couple of pubs for when you're ready to leave the window shopping behind.

fringe
www.studio108.org
fringe@studio108.org
Coffee & Craft
MAKE YOUR OWN FOREST FRIEND
ROWAN
Fat Quarters £2.50
Fat Quarters £4
DEWHURST'S 'SYLKO'

FRINGE

108 Alexandra Park Road Muswell Hill, London N10 2AE

Fringe is situated in picturesque Muswell Hill, not far from the famous Alexandra Palace (or Ally Pally as Londoners call it), home of the Knitting and Stitching Show that happens annually in October.

Walk inside and you find yourself in an art gallery. An art gallery with yarn and haberdashery, that is. There are regular exhibitions at Fringe, and one of the highlights of the 2014 Great London Yarn Crawl was the opportunity for participants to meet and talk with felt and textile artist Cathy Needham.

Fringe has a wide selection of products, ranging from lovely yarns to vintage buttons and haberdashery, to fabrics and sewing products. If you're feeling in the need for super instant gratification, you can buy handknit scarves, or pick up a kit for a sweater or some knitted jewelry if you've got a bit more patience.

The shop offers a range of classes and workshops – they have the standard beginning knit and crochet classes, but also offer classes on lace, colourwork, Intarsia and cables. Sewing classes include a beginner's quilting class, and classes for specific sewing projects. They've also got a selection of classes geared towards kids, including holiday workshops. Fringe also hosts "Meet and Make" social evenings on the first Wednesday of the month.

A paint-your-own-pottery place is located next door to Fringe and is a fun spot to visit with kids. ■

LOCAL TIP

Fringe is located on a block of friendly shops and restaurants all in a row. We particularly enjoyed Owen's, a lovely deli and cafe just a few doors up the road from Fringe.

Contact:
fringe108.london
admin@fringe108.london
020 8883 9478

Opening hours:
Monday – Friday: 9:30am – 5:30pm
Saturday: 10am – 5:30pm

LOOP

15 Camden Passage
Islington, London N1 8EA

Having recently celebrated their tenth anniversary, Loop is the Grande Dame of London's knitting scene.

Refined and elegant, there is an effortless chic to the shop that makes it as pretty as the wares within. Stocking an astonishing range of rare and hard-to-find brands from the States, the UK and the rest of the world, Loop is the UK flagship for Quince & Co yarns, and the only European stockist of Brooklyn Tweed Shelter and Loft. Other well known brands include Madelinetosh, Shalimar, Habu, Isager, Shibui, BC Garn, DyeForYarn, Cowgirlblues, Freia, Handmaiden, Kismet, Pigeonroof Studios and Wollmeise.

Loop has also championed many UK indie dyers, if you're looking to buy British. Some of the most popular, such as The Uncommon Thread and Eden Cottage Yarns, can be found on the shop's shelves, along with the gorgeous Shilasdair – hand dyed on the Isle of Skye – and Orkney Angoras from Scotland. If it's fair isle you fancy, there's a full selection of all of the colours of Jamieson's wool from Shetland.

A large selection of books and patterns for both knitting and crochet is tucked away upstairs next to a well-placed couch. The shop is well stocked with a variety of buttons and tools from ChiaoGoo, Clover, Sajou, Addi, Bryson, Tulip and Lacis, ribbons and vintage haberdashery, including Bakelite beehive yarn keepers and metal needle gauges.

Loop has a regular schedule of classes and workshops, and has hosted some amazing designers and teachers. Past workshops have been taught by Stephen West, Franklin Habit, Cirilia Rose, Aoibhe Ni, and Amy Hendrix. Check the shop's website to see what's happening when you're planning your visit.

Islington is a vibrant North London neighbourhood that boasts many fabulous shops and restaurants. Our faves include: Wahaca (a local London chain featuring Mexican street food), Kipferl (an Austrian cafe with excellent coffee and sausages, located right in Camden Passage), Ottolenghi (the original London location of the Israeli chef's restaurants), and The Angelic, a fab local pub tucked in a few streets over from the tube but worth the walk for the local brews on tap. Try and get the round nook upstairs for a view with lots of comfy pillows. ■

LOCAL TIP

If you're into vintage and antiques, Camden Passage features an antique market on Wednesdays and Saturdays. Many of the shops in Camden Passage also have a vintage connection, or feature handmade items. Take the time to wander and explore this gorgeous area - which is also prettily lit with Christmas lights from November onwards.

Contact:
loopknitting.com
shop@loopknitting.com
020 7288 1160

Opening hours:
Tuesday – Wednesday: 11am – 6pm
Thursday: 11am – 7:30pm
Friday – Saturday: 11am – 6pm
Sunday: 12pm – 6pm

NEST

102 Weston Park, Crouch End
London N8 9PP

Climb off the W3 bus from Finsbury Park station, wander down a lovely residential street and you will find Nest, a gorgeous shop tucked away in Crouch End.

Nest has injected new yarns, independent sewing patterns and fabrics into their repertoire. Yarns include Navia, Toft Alpacas, Erika Knight, SweetGeorgia, Fyberspates, BC Garn, Woolyknit, Rico, Debbie Bliss, Blacker Yarns, Stitch & Story and Adriafil, as well as their eponymous line of undyed yarns, Nest Naturals. Their sewing pattern lines include Little Woolie, Oliver + S children's patterns, Gather, Sew Me Something and Merchant & Mills.

Class offerings include sewing, dressmaking and knitting and crochet for both adults and children. They also offer crafty kids' parties. Additionally, Nest hold a library of craft books and resources for customers to borrow, and run knitting groups on Monday afternoons and in the evening on the first Friday of every month. Check their website or their Facebook page for updated class offerings and event times.

Contact:
nestknitting.com
info@nestknitting.com
020 8340 8852

Opening hours:
Monday - Friday: 11am - 6pm
Saturday: 10am - 6pm

LOCAL TIP

If you're travelling with a football fan, the Handweavers Studio & Gallery is a short walk from the Arsenal Football Stadium – maybe send the fans there while you have a good long browse?

Contact:
handweavers.co.uk
info@handweavers.co.uk
020 7272 1891

Opening hours:
Monday – Saturday:
10am – 6pm

THE HANDWEAVERS STUDIO & GALLERY

140 Seven Sisters Road London N7 7NS

If you are a weaver, or a knitter who thinks weaving might be interesting, or a yarn person who's flirted with the idea of starting to spin, the Handweavers Studio & Gallery is the shop for you.

Upon first entering, you're met by piles and piles of fibre for spinning or felting, ranging from dyed merino tops and silk, to natural coloured wools, to luxury fibres like alpaca, camel and cashmere, as well as plant fibres like milk and bamboo. The brilliant thing is that all the fibres are available to purchase in 25 gr increments – perfect if you find a fibre you've been wanting to try out.

Move past the fibre and the books to reach the yarn. Unlike a traditionally focused knitting shop, this yarn selection is curated for weaving; most of the yarns are on cones, and are classified by weaving conventions rather then by the more familiar "Aran" and "4-ply" terms. Since there are many ways to classify weaving yarns, it may be a bit confusing as to which yarn is a 4-ply, and what's a laceweight. Helpfully, many of the yarns have wpi/wpc (wraps per inch or wraps per cm) designations, which can help to steer you in the right direction. And when in doubt, ask a member of staff. The yarns cover a wide range from plant fibres (tencel, bamboo, rayon, viscose, cotton and linen) to wool, silk and even paper!

The library includes a wide range of books on many weaving topics, as well as spinning, felting, dyeing and knitting and crochet books. If you're really feeling brave, you can delve even further into the shop and check out their selection of looms, Ashford spinning wheels, and other tools.

The Handweavers Studio & Gallery offers a variety of well-attended and well-respected classes, including beginning and advanced weaving and introductory spinning. They also run a two year weaving course called the Handweavers Diploma, which gives weavers an opportunity to expand their skills. Whatever your fibre-y leanings, the Handweavers Studio & Gallery is sure to have something to pique your interest.

FABRICATIONS

7 Broadway Market
Hackney, London E8 4PH

Located in Hackney, near Regent's Canal, Fabrications houses an array of crafting supplies that speak to the owner's belief that craft can create positive change in the world.

Fabrications offers a selection of products that supports their passion for sustainable community and locally sourced materials. With commercial yarn and local handspun yarns, knitting accessories, sewing machines and notions, and a selection of upcycling kits, Fabrications has plenty to inspire and motivate your next crafting adventure.

Downstairs, Fabrications has an amazing class space where they hold workshops ranging from knitting and crochet classes, to hand and machine sewing, upcycling, feltmaking, weaving and spinning. Thursday evenings bring their Craft Club, which is open to crafters of all sorts. No matter your crafty identity, Fabrications has something for you!

LOCAL TIP

On Saturdays the Broadway Market comes to life with lots of food stalls and vendors selling their wares. This is a charming area to walk around and explore, or sit and watch the world go by from one of the many pubs and restaurants along the street.

Contact:
fabrications1.co.uk
textiles@fabrications1.co.uk
020 7275 8043

Opening hours:
Tuesday - Friday: 12pm - 5:30pm
Saturday: 10am - 5:30pm
Sunday: 12pm - 5pm

EAST
GIFT VOUCHERS
AVAILABLE!
facebook
Emotional
Baggage

KNIT WITH ATTITUDE

127 Stoke Newington High Street, London N16 0PH

One of the really exciting things about the variety of knitting shops in London is how they've all found ways to offer something different to yarn enthusiasts. Knit With Attitude is no exception. Their concept is simple: focus on eco-friendly and ethically minded yarns.

The stories behind the yarns and the reasons they are included in the shop are as varied as the products themselves. The yarns don't have to be organic or made in the UK to be included, and they are happy to explain the reasons for their choices (in fact, stories about many of the brands that KWA carries can be found on the shop's website if you're looking to do any pre-shopping research).

Support is shown for British brands such as Wool and the Gang, Susan Crawford, Fyberspates and Blacker Yarns, as well as independent dyer Kettle Yarn Co. Yarns from further afield include The Fibre Co., Nurturing Fibres, Anna's Angora and Manos del Uruguay.

Care is also taken with the selection of the items available in the haberdashery. The shelves hold everything from KnitPro needles, Soak and Cocoknits accessories to stitch markers and knitting-inspired ceramics by Annette Bugansky.

Knit With Attitude also hosts the Attitude School in the shop. Classes include customized knitting and crochet lessons, to specific classes on topics ranging from how to read patterns, to making acrylic jewellery and finishing techniques. There's also a monthly knit night on the third Thursday of the month, with a 10% discount off all yarns on the evening – check the website for the current schedule.

Contact:
knitwithattitude.com
sales@knitwithattitude.com
020 7998 3282

Opening hours:
Monday – Saturday: 10am – 6pm
Sunday: 12pm – 6pm

LOCAL TIP

Knit With Attitude shares its retail space with Of Cabbages and Kings - a shop devoted to promoting indie makers and artisans in Hackney and London. Wares include jewellery and illustrated prints, to posters, bags, notebooks, aprons and oven mitts. Of Cabbages and Kings is a great place to start if you're looking for a unique, handmade gift - whether for yourself or as a souvenir of your trip.

PRICK YOUR FINGER

Prick Your Finger describes itself as "a Yarn Shop and Textile Collective", and grew out of the owner's desire to make textiles with UK-based yarns.

It's a yarn shop and art gallery, with exhibits side by side with fantastic UK yarns you won't find anywhere else. Yarns range from handspun skeins to gorgeous overdyed English Romney, to Yorkshire Mohair to handspun Embroidery Thread from the Lake District. The shop has its own line of yarn in 4-ply, DK, Aran, and Chunky weights, as well as Excelana from Susan Crawford, Paint by Numbers from John Arbon, and a range of yarns from the Wensleydale Longwool Sheep Shop.

Beyond yarn, the shop offerings include a variety of tools, including darning mushrooms, handmade mini-niddy noddies and wooden knitting needles, and a great selection of vintage buttons and little gift-y items perfect for the yarn artist in your life. The shop offers classes and workshops with visiting artists. These range from beginner's knitting, crochet, tatting and macrame, to "Socks in time for Christmas!" and "Decoding the Knitting Pattern". Throughout, Prick Your Finger's commitment to the love of creation and environmental awareness comes through in everything they do.

Don't miss the cheeky "Moths are Wankers" buttons and stickers. They make great gifts for all the fibre-lovers in your life, especially if your suitcase is threatening to explode with souvenir yarn.

Sadly, Prick Your Finger closed their bricks-and-mortar shop in December of 2015, and moved online. However, there are plans for the shop to return in a new form in the future – please check the website for any new developments. ■

Contact:
prickyourfinger.com
info@prickyourfinger.com
(online only)

LOCAL TIP

Directly across Globe Road from Prick Your Finger, is The Larder, a vegan-friendly vegetarian café. With fantastic coffee and food, this lovely eatery is a high point on the Great London Yarn Crawl every year!

LOCAL TIP

Keep an eye out for Travelknitter and The Wool Kitchen yarns in the shop. Both are dyed locally in London and make for an excellent souvenir yarn purchase. Also be sure to check out the shop's upcoming events listings as Wild & Woolly features a monthly "lock-in" as well as other special events and classes in addition to their regular knit night.

WILD & WOOLLY

116 Lower Clapton Road London E5 0QR

One of the newest kids on the London yarn shop block, Wild & Woolly opened in the spring of 2014.

This yarn-filled gem in Hackney is a community shop providing supplies and support for all manner of knitters, and anyone else seeking new adventures with yarn. Wild & Woolly houses a carefully curated collection: the small space holds a surprising range of yarns from Baa Ram Ewe, Cascade, The Fibre Company, Jamieson's, Karin Oberg, Kettle Yarn Co., Lett Lopi, Navia, Noro, Rico Designs, Rooster, Schoppel Yarns, Town End Alpaca, Travelknitter, West Yorkshire Spinners, The Wool Kitchen, and Woolyknit – truly this covers the whole spectrum! The shop also carries kits and accessories, and some exclusive project bags.

Contact:
wildandwoollyshop.co.uk
info@wildandwoollyshop.co.uk
020 8985 5231

Opening hours:
Tuesday – Saturday: 10:30am – 6pm
Sunday: 12pm – 4:30pm

In addition to yarns, needles and notions, the shop offers classes in knit and crochet, as well as kid-friendly workshops. They've also come up with an ingenious way to help crafters get rid of excess unused yarn – the Stash Depot! Unused yarns can be added to the Stash Depot, and knitters earn 50% of the sale price, which can be collected as cash or used toward the purchase of new yarn. We know which one we'd pick!

LOCAL TIP

Around the corner from Herne Hill catch the 35 bus to Brixton station (you can also catch the train one stop to Brixton). The Brixton market is famous in London for its variety of food and value – the eats are excellent! On weekends the outdoor market usually changes theme every week but it's a great place to wander through the arcades and explore the myriad of shops and restaurants from around the world all tucked in together. There's usually some great African fabric shops and vintage finds too.

SHARP WORKS

220 Railton Road, Herne Hill London SE24 0JT

The first things you notice when you walk into Sharp Works are the vintage cinema chairs lining one wall. It's as if they say, yes, please do fold one down and place your things here so that you can have a proper browse in the shop!

Almost directly opposite the National Rail station in Herne Hill, Sharp Works is a small shop filled with a wide variety of yarns and notions that defy its size. Well known British brands abound, including Rowan, Louisa Harding, Debbie Bliss, but they also have Noro, Manos, Rico and Mirasol on offer. International brands such as Adriafil, Juniper Moon, Ella Rae and Navia Yarn from the Faroe Islands are also available.

Sharp Works operate a brisk business Wednesday through Saturday – the only days that the shop is open. They also teach a number of beginner and intermediate knitting and crochet classes – check their website for more details.

Contact:
sharpworks.co.uk
mail@sharpworks.co.uk
020 7738 7668

Opening hours:
Wednesday - Saturday 10:30 – 6pm

FABRIC

Sewing has seen a huge resurgence in the UK, in part fueled by the popularity of BBC programme The Great British Sewing Bee. Of course, we use the word 'resurgence' lightly! As crafters, we know how annoying it is to be told that our craft is on the upswing in popular culture when we've been making happily all along.

Fabric shops in London are filled with inspiration and gorgeous textures at every turn. Whatever your fancy, be it dressmaking or quilting or something else entirely, you're sure to have no trouble finding it. Keep an eye out for patterns by makers By Hand London and Tilly Walnes (Tilly and the Buttons, of Great British Sewing Bee fame) if you're looking for something local or if you're looking to meet up socially, the London Modern Quilt Guild gets together monthly.

The one thing we've noticed about fabric shops in London is that they tend to be grouped together in specific locations, making it much easier to visit a whole bunch at once. Take a look at what's grouped together but keep in mind that many of the shops are easily accessible by public transport.

BERWICK STREET

Running from the east end of Oxford Street, deep into Soho, Berwick Street is a road of sewist's sweet shops, and a regular haunt for costume designers for the West End theatres and the London film industry.

Not only fabric but every sort of accessory can be bought here: feathers in every colour, sparkly top hats and masks for fancy dress parties and rhinestones for skater and ballroom dancing costumes. Just walk east down Oxford Street from Tottenham Court Road Tube station and turn left when you reach Berwick Street. Don't worry, you won't see anything interesting at first, and you will have to dodge the white vans hurtling down the street to deliver fruit and vegetables to the market, but keep your eyes peeled and you will find exactly what you are looking for (or something equally beautiful).

Some shops (like Borovick Fabrics) have been in the street forever, others come and go, but there is always something new to see and explore. Watch out for tiny entrances, just a door's width, climb the rickety stairs to discover a shop over another shop. People are always welcome and they love to chat – they don't always get a lot of visitors up there! If you are not quite sure what you want, they might be able to help.

You will find everything you need for dressing up or the theatre, as well as your regular dressmaking. Not everything is on display – one wardrobe mistress, responsible for dressing one or two of the big West End shows, talks of rows and rows of plain brown boxes in one shop, each one containing bright ribbons and trims. You'll have to search out some of these things. Although the shops have websites, this is really a place for personal shopping.

LOCAL TIP

Berwick Street is also easily reached from Oxford Circus tube station if you've been exploring around Liberty and John Lewis. If you get tired while you're on your quest, there are plenty of cafes next to the shops, selling good tea and coffee and cakes.

14
THE BERWICK STREET
CLOTH SHOP
14

THE BERWICK STREET CLOTH SHOP

14 Berwick Street London W1F 0PP

At The Berwick Street Cloth Shop you will find silks, velvet, brightly coloured tweed, faux fur and pleather as part of their extensive and large selection of fabrics.

The shop also has a beautiful selection of bridal and eveningwear fabrics, as well as interior fabrics for soft furnishings. The Berwick Street Cloth Shop prides itself on supporting students in the fashion industry, and the friendly and helpful staff are very knowledgeable when it comes to the stock in their particular shop. They can usually be counted on to give you an idea of how much fabric you will need for standard clothing items and are endlessly patient with students from the nearby art colleges, who come in asking for fabric samples.

Contact:
theberwickstreetclothshop.com
sales@theberwickstreetclothshop.com
020 7287 2881

Opening hours:
Monday – Friday: 9am – 6pm
Saturday: 10am – 6pm

BOROVICK FABRICS

Berwick Street Market
16 Berwick Street
London W1F 0HP

Borovicks has stood at 16 Berwick Street in the market end of the street for more than 80 years. It is often a good place for bargains as well as good quality silks.

It is not just the place to go for yards of neon coloured tulle or animal print lycra (although both are available), but there are roll ends from the East End rag trade too. You can find leftover silk from Betty Jackson's workshops and rolls of men's shirting from Mr. Pink. You will find your lining there too, and the basics of haberdashery.

Walk past the burlesque and the remnants deep into the back of the shop and you will find plain-coloured silks in many weights and colours at very reasonable prices. The staff are friendly and their manners faintly reminiscent of the old days of Soho, when there was a garment factory on every corner and pedestrians had to dodge the delivery boys rushing around with wheelbarrows piled high with bolts of fabric.

Contact:
borovickfabrics.com
borovickfabrics@btclick.com
020 7437 2180

Opening hours:
Monday - Friday: 8:30am - 6pm
Saturday: 8:30am - 5pm

BOROVICK
16

tel/fax: 020 7437 5155
Cloth House
47
www.clothhouse.com

CLOTH HOUSE

47 Berwick Street London W1F 8SJ

Cloth House sells cotton, linen and a large selection of technical fabrics in the basement, as well as every sort of haberdashery.

As you walk in, if you can tear your eyes away from the wonderful and original window display, you will see racks of ribbons filling one wall. Every sort you could imagine and in every colour, all sold by the metre.

Further in the shop there are jars and jars of buttons, from tiny hand-made mother of pearl to giant plastic, leather and wood. Bolts of cotton and linen fabric in plains and patterns are all around. There are bargains to be had amongst the printed cottons but also a large selection of Japanese fabrics. If you see it and love it, buy it; like most of the shops in Berwick Street, the stock is not often repeated.

Contact:
clothhouse.com
47@clothhouse.com
020 7437 5155

Opening hours:
Monday – Friday: 9:30am – 6pm
Saturday: 10:30am – 6pm

THE SILK SOCIETY

Berwick Street Market
44 Berwick Street
London W1F 8SE

This is the shop you might visit to buy fabric for that once in a lifetime dress – your wedding dress perhaps, or for the smartest ball you will ever attend.

The silks are just wonderful; beaded, layered, and embroidered instead of plain. Mostly in muted colours, there are nevertheless some brights in there too. The stock and the window displays are a feast for the eyes. It is probably worth going in just to look and wonder. Or you could buy a meter or two to work in with a plainer silk, so don't be afraid to go in and explore!

Contact:
thesilksociety.com
sales@thesilksociety.com
020 7287 1881

Opening hours:
Monday – Friday: 9am – 6pm
Saturday: 10am – 6pm

SILK
TEL: 020 7287 1881
SECOM
THE
SILK
SOCIETY
43

JOHN LEWIS

Oxford Street
London W1C 1DX

Once the mecca of sewers throughout the south of England, the John Lewis home sewing department occupied almost the whole ground floor of its Oxford Street store.

The department shrank over time to a corner at the back of one of the upper floors. However, the department is again on the up. It stocks a reasonable supply of patchwork fabrics, including Amy Butler and Cath Kidston, and an increasing range of dress fabrics.

The haberdashery tends to be mostly pre-packed; they stock patterns from the main commercial producers including Vogue, Butterick and McCalls, but not the independents such as Collette and Lisette. They also offer a large number of sewing and knitting kits. Sewing machines by Singer, Bernina and Janome, as well as their own label, are available for purchase. The staff are knowledgeable and skilled in advising their customers on the right machine for the job (and the operator).

The yarn department is also growing, with commercial yarns including a large range of Rowan, Debbie Bliss, Erika Knight and Wendy, with suitable notions and patterns to match. Fabric and notions for soft furnishings such as curtains and chair covers are in a separate department, where the range remains strong.

John Lewis is a good place to source the basics for sewing and knitting, but for more unusual products, the crafter will still need to go elsewhere. The shop's website is everything you would expect from a modern business, well laid out, clear, informative and with an efficient delivery system.

Contact:
johnlewis.com
020 7629 7711

Opening hours:
Monday - Saturday: 9:30am - 8pm
Sunday: 12pm - 6pm

LIBERTY

Silk Satin

LIBERTY

Regent Street
London W1B 5AH

The Destination Shop to beat all destination shops. Liberty is best known for its iconic line of fabrics and prints.

We could chat about the pretty flower shop that hugs the entrance in its exotic scents, the wonderful costume jewelry, the handbags and the designer clothes, but we really want to share what Liberty has for crafters.

Most of their haberdashery comes in little kits, including ribbon in lengths of about 2 m. They have a large number of whole project sewing kits, such as everything you need to make a pincushion in Cath Kidston fabric, which would make good presents for new sewers. The choice of the iconic Liberty print Tana Lawn and fine wool fabrics is huge, and the recently introduced Art Fabrics fire the imagination with ideas for all sorts of projects. The knitting department carries the full Rowan range, and needles and patterns to go with the stock.

Liberty also have a small stand of Merchant & Mills notions and a limited range of ribbons and trims from V V Rouleaux. Finally Café Liberty on the second floor is a good place for weary shoppers to stop for afternoon tea.

Contact:
liberty.co.uk
020 7734 1234

Opening hours:
Monday – Saturday: 10am – 9pm
Sunday: 12pm – 6pm

LOCAL TIP

Feeling multi-craftual? Ray Stitch is a short five to ten minute walk from Loop. Head south towards Angel tube station along Essex Road and duck into Camden Passage. Also make sure to check out the Loop listing under Yarn for tips on local eateries and other key features in the area!

RAY STITCH

99 Upper Street
Islington N1 2SJ

Ray Stitch is small and perfectly formed. The shop is known for its small range of original dress fabrics, including some from Japan, and a large stock of interesting and original fabric for patchwork, as well as buttons, ribbons and trims.

They also carry upholstery and crafting materials. This is the ideal place to find all things haberdashery, with an extensive range of products from Prym, Clover and Merchant & Mills. From their large stock, you are bound to find exactly the right size hook and eye or snap fastener, packet of needles or pins. You can buy heavier duty fasteners and trims here too, suitable for soft furnishings.

Patterns stocked include Merchant & Mills, Colette, Deer and Doe, Simplicity, New Look, Minikrea and Oliver + S, with samples on display. The staff are helpful and friendly, and are clearly very interested in the products the shop has to sell.

Ray Stitch runs courses in all sorts of sewing activities, from introduction to machine sewing and dressmaking to pattern cutting and creative stitching at all levels. Its well-designed website is clear and bright, and if you can't get to the shop for the full Ray Stitch experience, shopping online is a good second best.

Contact:
raystitch.co.uk
info@raystitch.co.uk
020 7604 1060

Opening hours:
Monday: 10am – 4pm
Tuesday – Saturday: 9am – 6:30pm
Sunday: 11am – 5pm

The Village
HABERDASHERY
girls 10-up
make a
SKIRT!
tomorrow
10am-12.30pm
Come In
OPEN

SINGER

NORTH

THE VILLAGE HABERDASHERY

47 Mill Lane
London NW6 1NB

The Village Haberdashery is much more than a fabric store. They provide supplies for crafters who knit, crochet, sew, quilt, embroider and more!

Their fabrics are amazing, including such brands as Cotton + Steel and some Japanese Kokka fabrics, as well as Liberty, Moda and Sevenberry. They also have a wide range of notions and haberdashery, as you might expect from the name, including bag and belt hardware, cushions and kits in addition to the expected ribbons, buttons and trims.

The Village Haberdashery also offer a wide variety of classes for a range of crafts and skill levels. For sewists, there are quilting classes and dressmaking, as well as classes and workshops for kids. There are also a number of fabric clubs available, from the Baby Quilt Club to the Colour of the Month Club to help boost your fabric stash. Check out the website for update class offerings and times.

Originally begun as a fabric shop, The Village Haberdashery continues to expand their yarn selections. They stock The Fibre Co., Artesano, Cascade, Madeleinetosh, Spud & Chloe, Blue Sky Alpacas, Stitch & Story and Toft yarns, as well as a range of classes for knitters.

Contact:
thevillagehaberdashery.co.uk
info@thevillagehaberdashery.co.uk
020 7794 5635

Opening hours:
Monday – Saturday: 10am – 5pm
Sunday: 11am – 5pm

FABRICS GALORE

52-54 Lavender Hill
London SW11 5RH

South of the river away from the main fabric hubs of the city is Fabrics Galore, a decent-sized fabric shop on the edge of Battersea and Clapham.

The shop has everything you could possibly want and more: fabrics for dressmaking, patchwork and soft furnishings, including oilcloth and Libery Art fabrics, as well as all of the accompanying notions.

While the shop is a good size and well lit, once you're past the novelty, quilting, Liberty and oilcloth options that are near the front of the shop, the rest of the shop can be a bit overwhelming with everything that's in there! This is a great place to come for inspiration, and then stay to make your purchases, as the prices are more than reasonable - especially when measured against prices north of the river.

Fabrics Galore also takes a stand at a few of the larger knitting and stitching shows around the country over the course of the year where you can find some fabulous deals.

Contact:
fabricsgalore.co.uk
info@fabricsgalore.co.uk
020 7738 9589

Opening hours:
Monday - Saturday: 9:30am - 6pm

FABRICS
GALORE
SOUTH

haart
SEW
OVER
IT
78
OPEN

LEAR
TO S W
WITH US
SALE!

SEW OVER IT

Clapham: 78 Landor Road, London SW9 9PH

Islington: 36A Myddelton Street, London EC1R 1UA

Originally founded in Clapham, Sew Over It expanded their sewing studio and café empire with the opening of a shop in Islington in late 2014. These shops are tiny little havens of creativity devoted to introducing as many people to sewing as possible, and designed to encourage people to connect with sewing again.

Cleverly, the sewing café promises "unlimited cups of tea" for £6/hour and the use of the shop's Janome sewing machines and overlockers. Familiarity with the machines is required, and experienced sewists can benefit from the wider space and large tables to work on – more than one might be used to in a London flat!

For those who are new to sewing, Sew Over It has a huge array of classes across beginning sewing, quilting and dressmaking, as well as accessories, for the home and pattern cutting. They've also thoughtfully rated their classes, so that you can determine if your skills will measure up to those needed in a particular class.

The Sewing Café only happens one day a week at each location. The rest of the time there may be classes happening, so it's a good idea to check the website when planning your visit.

Contact:
sewoverit.co.uk
info@sewoverit.co.uk
020 7326 0376 (Clapham)
020 7833 8600 (Islington)

Clapham opening hours:
Tuesday – Friday: 10am – 6pm
Saturday: 10am – 5pm
Sunday: 10am – 3pm

Islington opening hours:
Tuesday – Friday: 1pm – 6pm
Saturday: 12pm – 5pm

SHAUKAT & COMPANY

170 – 172 Old Brompton Road London SW5 0BA

A serious fabric shop for serious sewists, Shaukat features a very large selection of fabric, but little else.

They stock almost the full range of Liberty fabrics, including wools and silks as well as cotton lawns. In fact, they carry so much Liberty fabric, that there is more on display here than in Liberty itself!

Shaukat's own ranges of printed cottons is huge, and they stock luxury fibre blends too, such as light as a feather silk cotton. Although most of the fabric they stock is patterned, much of it traditional florals, they also have a good range of plain fabrics in poplin, silk and velvet. Just leave yourself lots of time for your visit. Shaukat's website is comprehensive, but fabric samples are small and it is better to shop in person unless you know exactly what you want.

LOCAL TIP

If you're a big fan of Liberty fabrics, or a quilter looking for smaller quantities, Shaukat is a better shop to visit than Liberty for a few reasons. The minimum cut here is half a meter, as opposed to one meter at Liberty. Shaukat also has remnant scraps that are a treasure trove of some of the most iconic Liberty prints. Depending on the size, the scraps run anywhere from £2-5. Perfect for small bits for hand sewing or English Paper Piecing.

Contact:
shaukat.co.uk
info@shaukat.co.uk
020 7373 6927

Opening hours:
Monday - Saturday: 10am - 7pm

FAX 020 7373 5516
Shaukat Fabrics
WEST
Fabrics

GOLDHAWK ROAD

Hammersmith, London W12

More like an open air bazaar than a series of fabric shops, this is the street where you can find bargains. Shops display their many rolls of fabric in overflowing bins on the pavement (on fine days only!).

Shopkeepers along Goldhawk Road can be unusually enthusiastic, pouncing on anyone who shows an interest in their wares. Beware, not all bargains are what they seem.

The really good deals can be found in last year's designs from big labels, if you don't mind out-of-season patterns. You may also find good plain silks and woolen fabric, but know what you're looking for, and be familiar with the full prices for goods, if you're looking for a good deal.

We recommend you also check the fibre content carefully, and don't rely on vague descriptions. If the label says "fibre of unknown content" it may not be the fabric you're looking for. Despite all these warnings, Goldhawk Road is a fun place for the seasoned crafter to spend an afternoon.

LOCAL TIP

Head to the Goldhawk Road Station on the Hammersmith & City Tube line for easy access to Goldhawk Road fabrics.

HABERDASHERY

You've got your yarn or your fabric, but what about buttons? What about grosgrain ribbon or the perfect zipper? Handles for a bag? Beads?

In this section, we cover the fabulous and fantastic haberdasheries that London has available. These shops are treasure troves of the sparkly, the beautiful and the perfect final touch for your special project.

BEADWORKS

21a Tower Street
Seven Dials, Covent Garden
London WC2H 9NS

Down a little side street from Covent Garden's famous Seven Dials is Beadworks, a huge shop for the tiny treasures that are displayed inside.

For beading and jewelry-making crafters, if you were only to visit one bead shop on your trip to London, we'd recommend this one. Row upon row of beads in every shape, colour and size imaginable can be found in this shop, along with findings, thread, wires and whatever other accessories you might require.

If you're looking for added sparkle you can also find Swarovski Elements products here and the shop has done a good job of having some of their stock available in small bags for better value than if purchasing individually.

For knitters, there are a wide variety of colours and sizes of seed beads, as well as Japanese Miyuki beads that make beautiful embellishments for lace shawls. Nothing compares to being able to pick a colour in person as opposed to online, so make sure you've got your project with you when you come for a visit.

Contact:
beadworks.co.uk
customerservice@beadworks.co.uk
020 7240 0931

Opening hours:
Monday – Saturday: 10:30am – 7pm

CENTRAL

MACCULLOCH & WALLIS

25-26 Poland Street
London W1F 8QN

Now based in Poland Street, MacCulloch & Wallis has been in providing fine fabrics and trims to the fashion industry since 1902. A wide range of fabric is available, although many people visit the shop for everything other than fabric.

Here you will find every sort and size of fastening, including zip fasteners by the meter, just measure the length you want, slide down one of the multiple heads and cut to size. They have a huge supply of sewing thread in different colours, grades and fibres. In addition to ribbons galore, there is a great range of lace trims and inserts. Their range of trimmings and braids include many suitable for soft furnishings and upholstery, and most stock items can be bought online.

In addition to haberdashery and fabric, MacCulloch & Wallis carry everything needed for millinery, including all the materials as well as preblocked hat bases, ready to trim. They also sell most equipment a sewer might want, including eyelets (and the tools to insert them), good quality scissors and the complete range of Bernina sewing machines; they also do machine servicing.

Contact:
macculloch-wallis.co.uk
samples@macculloch.com
020 7629 0311

Opening hours:
Monday – Wednesday: 10am – 6pm
Thursday: 10am – 7pm
Friday: 10am – 6pm
Saturday: 10:30am – 5pm

M^C CULLOCH & WALLIS L^TD
Est. 1902
Fabrics
M^C CULLOCH & WALLIS L^TD
Haberdashery
OPEN

ULSTRODE
TREET W1
OF WESTMINSTER
V V Rouleaux
2012

V V ROULEAUX

102 Marylebone Lane London W1U 2QD

V V Rouleaux only sells ribbons and trims, but what ribbons and trims! The variety is huge; satin, grosgrain, flock, gold threaded, spotted, striped, and in every colour of the rainbow.

There are flowers and bows and seasonal decorations too. In common with several of the shops profiled in this book, this is a destination shop – even if you don't actually need any ribbon or a silk rose, you will love looking around. We defy you to come out without buying a little something.

The V V Rouleaux website gives a good flavour of what you will find on your visit. You can shop online but nothing compares to checking out the merchandise in person.

Contact:
vvrouleaux.com
marylebone@vvrouleaux.com
020 7224 5179

Opening hours:
Monday – Tuesday: 9:30am – 6pm
Wednesday: 10:30am – 6pm
Thursday: 9:30am – 6:30pm
Friday – Saturday: 9:30am – 6:30pm

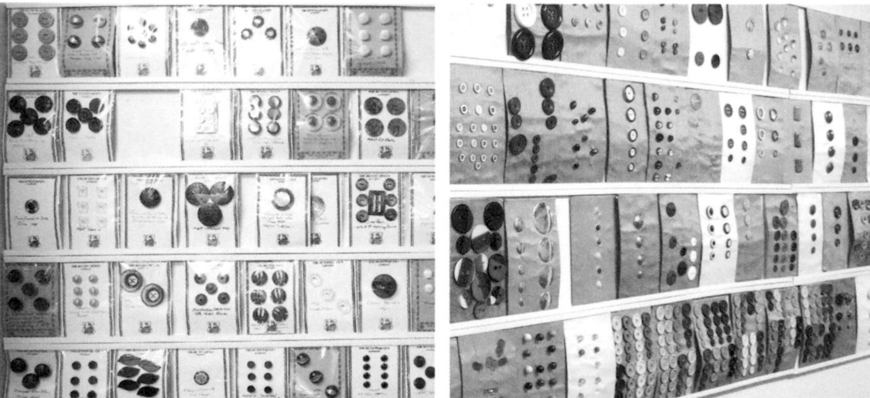

LOCAL TIP

It's an easy walk to this shop from busy Oxford Street, and we encourage you to use the tiny pedestrian passage from Oxford Street that is marked St. Christopher's Place. Once the passage opens up you're on a marvelous side street with many restaurants and cafes that are filled with patio tables when the weather is fine.

Marylebone is also a gorgeous area to walk around in and the window shopping is excellent. Once you've finished at The Button Queen, continue heading north towards Regent's Park where the gardens are gorgeous for sitting and knitting, or just enjoying with a leisurely stroll.

THE BUTTON QUEEN

76 Marylebone Lane London W1U 2PR

This tiny shop at the beginning of Marylebone Lane sells only buttons. They have every sort, from tiny mother-of-pearl shirt buttons sold in large packets to individual, antique buttons that are a thing of beauty in themselves.

This old family business, begun in the early 1960s, came to rest in Marylebone Lane nearly 40 years ago.

The shop has some lovely antique buttons, ideal for today's vintage style dresses and knits (most of which the shop advises are not to be washed), as well as modern easy care buttons that will not object to a turn in the washing machine. If you buy from them, particularly if you buy the old buttons, they will advise on how to care for them properly.

While the shop has a website, it is advisable to visit and shop in person, unless you know exactly what you want. The stock in the shop is much larger and the staff can often find treasures hidden away.

Contact:
thebuttonqueen.co.uk
information@thebuttonqueen.co.uk
020 7935 1505

Opening hours:
Monday – Friday: 10am – 5:30pm
Saturday: 10am – 3pm

THE LONDON BEAD CO.

339 Kentish Town Road London NW5 2TJ

Easily accessible from the Northern line, and literally right across the street from Kentish Town Station. The London Bead Co. is very much an allsorts kind of haberdashery.

The shop carries much more than their wide and varied selection of beads. Through a doorway at the back is Delicate Stitches, their sister shop with which they share space. If cross stitch, embroidery or hand stitching is your thing, you should find most if not all of what you seek here.

Alongside DMC and Anchor are specialty hand dyed wools and threads from Weeks Dye Works, The Thread Gatherers, Au Ver A Soie, Threadworx and Caron's Threads. Fabrics include everything from blanketing to Swiss cotton for smocking.

The shop also carries Swarovski Elements crystals and beads, as well as ribbons from Silks, Hanah Hand Dyed and Mokuba. There are also findings, books, tools and general haberdashery.

Contact:
londonbeadco.co.uk
info@londonbeadco.co.uk
020 7267 9403

Opening hours:
Monday – Saturday: 9:30am – 5:30pm

STAG & BOW

8 Dartmouth Road
London SE23 3XU

It's a bit of a jaunt from central London to get out to Stag & Bow, but what treats and treasures you'll find when you get there!

This friendly shop is a hodge-podge and celebration of making and sharing skills, seen and felt in the atmosphere of the shop as you're wandering amongst their haberdashery, yarn, and dressmaking supplies.

Stag & Bow are keen supporters of their community and feature many local makers whose works can be seen and purchased in the shop. They also offer a wide variety of workshops, many of which are beyond the usual "learn to knit and sew" formula. Check out their website to see what's on offer - their embroidery classes and lino print workshops were just a few that got us excited!

Contact:
stagandbow.com
info@stagandbow.com
020 8291 4992

Opening hours:
Tuesday – Saturday 10am - 5pm
Sunday 11am - 4pm

SINGER
COTTON
COTTON
COTTON
KNITTING NEEDLES

WIMBLEDON SEWING MACHINE CO.

292-312 Balham High Road London SW17 7AA

The Wimbledon Sewing Machine Company is one of those places that you might not seek out until you absolutely need to, and when you do, you'll wonder why you've never been before.

With the wide variety of supplies available, it's the perfect spot to start if you've got a fancy dress or other costume-centred event to make something for.

We've included the shop in the haberdashery section because of the depth and breadth of items that they carry. Not only is there fabric for dressmaking and quilting, but you can find fabric dyes and paints and patterns from seven major brands. The shop also carries yarn ranging from wool and wool blends to acrylic and fashion yarns, and knitting and crochet notions.

The shop has a wide range of equipment for cake decorating, as well as a tin hire, and offers cake decorating workshops along with their other craft and sewing classes.

As the name would suggest, you can also find sewing machines here. Perhaps the most delightful surprise is that the shop is also home to the London Sewing Machine Museum which opens on the first Saturday of the month. Admission is free although they suggest making a donation to their chosen charities. The crown of the collection is a rare sewing machine once owned by Queen Victoria's eldest daughter!

Contact:
craftysewer.com
wimbledonsewingmachinecoltd@btinternet.com
sewingandcraftsuperstore@btinternet.com
020 8767 4724 (sewing machine queries)
020 8767 0036 (craft queries)

Opening hours:
Monday, Tuesday, Thursday:
9am – 5:20pm
Wednesday: 9:15am – 5:20pm
Friday: 9am – 4:50pm

LYNDON'S STITCH & BEADS

197 Portobello Road London W11 2ED

If you're going to be exploring Notting Hill and the various shops along Portobello Road then chances are good you'll happen across Lyndon's Stitch & Beads.

This quirky little shop harkens back to a day when haberdashery shops weren't as specialized in one particular area as they are now. In fact, Lyndon's Stitch & Beads seems to have mostly a little bit of everything. Although the emphasis is definitely on beads and stitching such as cross stitch, you can also find a wide selection of ribbon, jewelry fastenings, rhinestones, buttons and general crafty paraphernalia.

LOCAL TIP

Be sure to check out the Portobello Road website to see the schedule of their rotating markets. Depending on the day, the market may be full of antiques, vintage fashion, second hand goods or fruit and veg.

portobelloroad.co.uk

Contact:
habercrafts.com
sales@habercrafts.com
020 7727 4357

Opening hours:
Monday – Saturday:
9:30am – 5:30pm
Sunday: 11am – 4pm

THE BEAD & JEWELLERY SHOP

95 Crown Road, St Margarets East Twickenham TW1 3EX

Heading west out of the city you'll find The Bead & Jewellery Shop in the charming neighbourhood of St Margarets, just east of Twickenham.

The shop has been in the area for over 20 years, capping the end of a picturesque street lined with cafes and shops.

While the shop is tiny, there is a solid selection of beads, kits, tools and findings as well as fused glass jewellery and gift items. Being a jewellery shop, they also do necklace restringing as well as other minor repairs. This is the perfect shop to go to for beads for that special lace shawl.

Contact:

thebeadandjewelleryshop
@btconnect.com
020 8891 4920

Opening hours:
Tuesday – Saturday: 10am – 6pm

DAY TRIPS

There are a number of cities within easy reach of London that have fabulous yarn and fabric offerings. We've collected a few of the best options including the historic university cities of Cambridge and Oxford, the hip seaside town of Brighton and the Roman stronghold of Bath. All are easily reached by train from central London within a couple of hours, and all have a selection of wonderful shops to visit, as well as many other sights to enjoy!

NORTH

Cambridge

This historic university city is located on the River Cam in Cambridgeshire, north of London. Most visitors come to see Cambridge University, one of the oldest in the world, and its stunning architecture. If the weather is fine, take a punting tour along the Cam to get an alternate view of the colleges from the river.

Sew Creative

58 King Street
Cambridge CB1 1LN
sewcreative.co.uk
cambridge@sewcreative.co.uk
012 2335 0691

Opening hours:
Monday – Saturday:
9am – 5pm

The Sheep Shop

72 Beche Road
Cambridge CB5 8HU
sheepshopcambridge.co.uk
sarah@sheepshopcambridge.co.uk
012 2331 1268

Opening hours:
Tuesday – Saturday: 10am – 6pm
(closed 2pm – 3pm)
Late opening Tuesday: 7pm
or 9pm on Knit Nights

Oxford

Home to Oxford University, the oldest university in the English-speaking world, the city is an easy one to walk and enjoy. Steeped in history from the time of the Saxons, keep your eyes peeled for architectural details such as the city's famous gargoyles, or the 14th century timber-framed building at the top of Cornmarket Street that looks like it's leaning right into the road. If time for a longer lunch allows, we recommend the Turl Street Kitchen.

Darn It & Stitch

Blue Boar Street
Oxford OX1 1DL
darnitandstitch.com
shop@darnitandstitch.com
018 6524 2779

Opening hours:
Monday – Saturday:
10am – 6pm
Sunday: 12 – 4pm

Oxford Yarn Store

3 North Parade Avenue
Oxford OX2 6LX
oxfordyarnstore.co.uk
info@oxfordyarnstore.co.uk
018 6560 4112

Opening hours:
Monday – Saturday:
10am – 6pm
Late opening Thursday:
10am – 8pm

SOUTH

Brighton

This hip, seaside town is a popular destination in the UK, for visitors ranging from families coming to the beach to hen parties and stag do's. Aside from checking out the wonderful sea front and iconic Brighton pier, our favourite thing to do in Brighton is to get lost wandering the Lanes. The heart of Brighton, the Lanes are an excellent spot for people-watching, as well as for finding all kinds of vintage, antique or brand new things in its many shops. The Lanes are also home to the crafty shops we've noted below, and it's worth mentioning that the pub found opposite yarn shop YAK is excellent.

Brighton Sewing Centre

68 North Road
Brighton BN1 1YD
brightonsewingcentre.co.uk
info@brightonsewingcentre.co.uk
012 7362 1653

Opening hours:
Monday – Saturday:
9:30am – 5:30pm

Ditto Fabrics

21 Kensington Gardens
Brighton BN1 4AL
dittofabrics.co.uk
sales@dittofabrics.co.uk
012 7360 3771

Opening hours:
Monday – Saturday:
11am – 5:30pm

YAK – Yarn and Knitting

16 Gloucester Road
Brighton BN1 4AD
yarnandknitting.com
yak@yarnandknitting.com
012 7367 9726

Opening hours:
Tuesday – Saturday:
10am – 6pm
Sunday: 11am – 4pm

Faversham

Located in the picturesque countryside of Kent, Faversham is a market town not far from Canterbury and another lovely seaside destination, Whitstable, that pre-dates Roman times. The building that houses yarn shop The Old Pharmacy is said to be from 1240.

The Old Pharmacy: Luxury Yarn Dispensary

6 Market Place, Faversham,
Kent ME13 7AG
theoldpharmacyfaversham.co.uk
gillian@theoldpharmacyfaversham.co.uk
017 9559 7700

Opening hours:
Tuesday, Friday & Saturday: 9am – 5pm
Wednesday: 10am – 5pm
Thursday: 1pm – 5pm
(Knit Night 7pm – 9pm)
Sunday: 10am – 3pm

WEST

Bath

Thanks to our Christmas Craft Crawl excursions, Bath is the daytrip destination we know best. This former Roman stronghold draws visitors to its famous Abbey, Roman baths and temple. Bath was also home to Jane Austen and fans of her work can visit the Jane Austen Centre. We highly recommend the Fashion Museum to see examples of Georgian dress, as well as more modern pieces.

Should you be visiting Bath at the end of November or beginning of December, you'll want to visit the Bath Christmas Market – one of the most authentic German-style Christmas markets in the UK. Upscale pub Hall & Woodhouse is a great place to have a pint and rest your feet after a long day of sightseeing.

A Yarn Story

128 Walcot Street, Bath BA1 5BG
ayarnstory.co.uk
carmen@ayarnstory.co.uk
012 2542 9239

Opening hours:
Monday – Saturday: 10am – 5pm

Bijoux Beads

Elton House, 2 Abbey Street, Bath BA1 1NN
bijouxbeads.co.uk
info@bijouxbeads.co.uk
012 2548 2024

Opening hours:
Monday – Saturday: 9:30am – 5:30pm
Sundays: 11am – 4:30pm
(check website for seasonal hours)

Country Threads

2 Pierrepont Place
Bath BA1 1JX
countrythreadspatchwork.co.uk
shop@countrythreadspatchwork.co.uk
012 2548 0056

Opening hours:
Monday – Saturday:
9:30am – 5pm

Wool

18 Old Orchard Street
Bath BA1 1JU
www.woolbath.co.uk
012 2546 9144

Opening hours:
Monday – Saturday:
9:30am – 5:30pm

The Makery

Beau Nash House
19 Union Passage
Bath BA1 1RD
themakery.co.uk
shop@themakery.co.uk
012 2558 1888

Opening hours:
Wednesday – Saturday:
10am – 5pm
Sunday: 11am – 4pm

PROJECTS

Being on holiday is a glorious opportunity for collecting memorable souvenirs of the places we visit. As crafters, very often those souvenirs come in the form of beautifully dyed wools or gorgeous fabrics we can't find at home.

With the idea of souvenir crafting in mind, we asked our designers to come up with the perfect souvenir projects, particularly ones that use only a skein or two of yarn or small amounts of fabric.

There are a couple of quicker Aran weight projects, as well as shawls, socks and fingerless mitts. The designs run the gamut from knitting to crochet to sewing, and can be worked up before, during or after your trip.

Inspired by iconic tourist destinations such as the London Eye and Eiffel Tower, we hope you'll enjoy the selection, and cast on if the inspiration takes you while still on your trip. Happy crafting!

BECAUSE SOCK YARN

By Kate Atherley

Sock yarn isn't really stash. It's only one skein. It's less than £20. It doesn't take up a lot of room in your bag. There's no worry about dye lots or yardage or gauge. It's just Sock Yarn. You have to buy it. It's a souvenir: a colourway evocative of the city. A colourway you've never seen before. It matches your coat.

And it's only one skein.

So how about using that one-of-a-kind beautiful souvenir skein for something that's as fun to knit as socks, but isn't for your feet? Use it for things you can show off.

Fingerless mitts. Specifically, fingerless mitts that are ideal for wearing while knitting in transit: whether on the way back from your trip, or just on your commute to work.

And because fingerless mitts don't use up much of the skein – and on their own aren't that interesting for a "souvenir" project – a matching shawlette. Although the two items are a set, they're not too matchy-matchy.

The mitts are designed with practicality in mind: they are fitted, and small. Small enough to not interfere if you wear them while knitting; small enough to fit under a pair of full mittens if you need the extra warmth. They're worked cuff up, in the round on your usual sock needles.

The shawlette is worked second, with whatever yarn you have leftover from the mittens. It's designed simply: start at one side with a small number of stitches and work until you've run out of yarn. A slow increase rate keeps the pieces narrow but long enough to wrap around your neck.

The shape and the edging keeps the knitting interesting but not too challenging. This motif is bold enough to stand up to the busiest of colourways – but looks just as good in something plainer.

Materials:

Indigodragonfly CaribouBaa, 1 skein in Bronte's Inferno
Fingering weight; 398 m per 115 g skein;
100% superwash Merino

Notes

If you want to make both items, make the mitts first, and then work the scarf with the leftovers, as the scarf easily adapts to any yardage.

For the mittens, you can vary the ribbing. The instructions specify the classic (k2, p2), but (k1, p1) works nicely, and you can also use a more decorative faux-cable ribbing, such as:

Faux cable ribbing Rnd 1:
(K2, p2) around.
Faux cable ribbing Rnd 2:
[Skip first st (leaving it in place on the needle) and k into second st (leaving it on the left needle), then k into first st, slip both off the needle at the same time, p2] around.
Faux cable ribbing Rnds 3 & 4:
(K2, p2) around.

Mittens

Needles
2.5 mm needles for working small circumferences in the round – DPNs, 1 long circular or 2 short circulars, as preferred

Gauge
34 sts x 48 rnds = 10 cm measured over St st

Other Supplies
stitch markers
a length of smooth scrap yarn in a contrasting colour for use as a stitch holder

Sizing
XXS (XS, S, M, L, XL)
To fit small teens to large men.
Hand circumference: 14 (15, 16.5, 18, 19, 20) cm
Length: 14.4 (15, 16.5, 17, 18, 18.5) cm; adjustable
Choose a size with a circumference a cm or two smaller than your actual hand circumference. The mitts should fit snugly.

Pattern

Cuff
Using a stretchy method like the Long Tail or Twisted German Cast On methods, and needles for working in the round, cast on 36 (40, 44, 48, 52, 56) sts. Distribute sts across needles as you prefer and join for working in the rnd.pm to mark beg of rnd.

Ribbing Rnd: *K2, p2; rep from * to end.

Work ribbing as set until cuff measures 5 (5, 5.5, 6, 6.5, 6.5) cm.

Next Rnd, inc for hand, size XXS only:
(K3, m1) 12 times - 48 sts.
Next Rnd, inc for hand, size XS only:
(K3, m1, k3, m1, k4, m1) 4 times - 52 sts.
Next Rnd, inc for hand, size S only:
(K3, m1, k4, m1, k4, m1) 4 times - 56 sts.
Next Rnd, inc for hand, size M only:
(K4, m1) 12 times - 60 sts.
Next Rnd, inc for hand, size L only:
(K4, m1, k4, m1, k5, m1) 4 times - 64 sts.
Next Rnd, inc for hand, size XL only:
(K4, m1, k5, m1, k5, m1) 4 times - 68 sts.

Thumb Gusset
Rnd 1, place markers and start inc: K1,pm, k1,pm, k to end of rnd - 1 st for thumb gusset.
Rnd 2, inc: K to marker, sm, m1R, k to next marker, m1L, sm, k to end of rnd - 2 sts inc in gusset.
Rnd 3: Knit.

Rep the last 2 rnds 1 (2, 1, 2, 3, 4) more times - 5 (7, 5, 7, 9, 11) gusset sts.

Work the inc rnd followed by 2 even rnds 6 (6, 8, 8, 8, 8) times - 17 (19, 21, 23, 25, 27) sts for gusset – 64 (70, 76, 82, 88, 94) sts.

Next rnd, separate thumb: K1, remove marker, slip next 17 (19, 21, 23, 25, 27) sts to scrap yarn; remove second marker, cast on 1 st over gap using the backwards loop method, k to end of round - 48 (52, 56, 60, 64, 68) sts.

Hand
Knit even until hand measures 2.5 cm from thumb opening – or to desired length before upper ribbing.

Decrease for ribbing: [K10 (11, 12, 13, 14, 15), k2tog] 4 times - 44 (48, 52, 56, 60, 64) sts.
Ribbing: *K2, p2; rep from * to end.
Work ribbing as set for 2 (2, 2.5, 2.5, 2.5, 2.5) cm.
Cast off in ribbing.

Thumb
Return held thumb sts to needles. With RS facing, rejoin yarn, and pick up and knit 3 sts in the gap over the cast on stitch of the hand, k to end of thumb sts - 20 (22, 24, 26, 28, 30) sts. Distribute sts and join for working in the rnd.pm to mark beg of rnd.
Rnd 1, sizes XS, M and XL only: K2, k2tog, k to 1 st before end of rnd, k2tog the last st of the rnd and the first st of the rnd - 20 (20, 24, 24, 28, 28) sts.
Rnd 1, sizes XXS, S and L only: Knit.

Ribbing: *K2, p2; rep from * to end.
Work ribbing as set for 2 (2, 2.5, 2.5, 2.5, 2.5) cm.
Cast off in ribbing.

Finishing
Block and weave in ends, closing up any holes at the base of the thumb.

Shawl

Needles
3.5 mm needles for working flat – straight or short circular

Gauge
21 sts x 40 rows (20 ridges) = 10 cm measured over G st
Matching gauge is not vital, but working at a different gauge will affect your yarn usage.

Other Supplies
stitch markers
tools for blocking: a surface you can pin the shawl to, and pins

Sizing
One. Sample as photographed measures 28 cm deep by 142 cm wide. Using more yarn will result in a larger piece; using less yarn will result in a smaller piece.

Pattern
Make a slipknot to cast on 1 st.

Set up Row (RS): Kfb - 2 sts.

Body of Shawl
Row 1 (RS): Kfb, k to marker, work Lace pattern Row 1 to end from chart or written instructions - 1 body st inc.
Row 2 (WS): Work Lace pattern Row 2, k to end.
Row 3: K to marker, work Lace pattern Row 3 to end.
Row 4: Work Lace pattern Row 4, k to end.
Row 5: K to marker, work Lace pattern Row 5 to end.
Row 6: Work Lace pattern Row 6, k to end.
Row 7: K to marker, work Lace pattern Row 7 to end.
Row 8: Work Lace pattern Row 8, k to end.
Row 9: Kfb, k to marker, work Lace pattern Row 9 to end - 1 body st inc.
Row 10: Work Lace pattern Row 10, k to end.
Row 11: K to marker, work Lace pattern Row 11 to end.
Row 12: Work Lace pattern Row 12, k to end.
Row 13: K to marker, work Lace pattern Row 13 to end.
Row 14: Work Lace pattern Row 14, k to end.
Row 15: K to marker, work Lace pattern Row 15 to end.
Row 16: Work Lace pattern Row 16, k to end.

Repeat these 16 rows until approximately 10 g of yarn remain, ending after Row 16.

Row 1 (WS): Knit.
Row 2: Kfb, k to last st - 1 st inc.
Repeat Rows 1 & 2 nine more times - 12 sts.
Final row (WS): K10,pm, k2.

Setup for Final Edging
The final section of the shawl is worked as an attached edging across the garter st portion of the shawl.

Count your sts. You need to cast on sts here for the final edging. The number to cast on is set by the number of sts you have. You need a multiple of 8 sts plus 11: any of 19, 27, 35, 43, 51, 59, 67, 75, 83, 91, 99... You need to get to the nearest of these numbers that is larger then the number of sts you have.

Using the cable cast on method, cast on the required number of sts at the start of the row. Then work the set up row.
Set up Row (WS): K10,pm, k2tog, turn.
The k2tog turns the corner, and joins the edging to the body of the shawl.

Row 1 (RS): K1, work Lace pattern Row 1 to end.
Row 2 (WS): Work Lace pattern Row 2 to m, sm, k2tog, turn.
Continue as set, working k2tog at the end of each WS row, until all sts of the shawl have been decreased away; on final WS row, cast off all rem sts.

Finishing
Wet block, pinning out the points of the edging. Weave in ends when dry.

Note for cast off on Row 16: you are binding off 8 sts; there should be 10 edging sts remaining when the cast off is complete, including the st on the right needle.

Lace Pattern Written Instructions
Row 1 (RS): (Yo, k2tog) 4 times, yo, k2 - 11 sts.
Row 2 and all WS rows unless otherwise stated: Knit.
Row 3: K1, (yo, k2tog) 4 times, yo, k2 - 12 sts.
Row 5: K2, (yo, k2tog) 4 times, yo, k2 - 13 sts.
Row 7: K3, (yo, k2tog) 4 times, yo, k2 - 14 sts.
Row 9: K4, (yo, k2tog) 4 times, yo, k2 - 15 sts.
Row 11: K5, (yo, k2tog) 4 times, yo, k2 - 16 sts.
Row 13: K6, (yo, k2tog) 4 times, yo, k2 - 17 sts.
Row 15: K7, yo, k10 - 18 sts.
Row 16: Bind off 8 sts, (1 st rem on right needle), k9 – 10 sts.

Lace Pattern

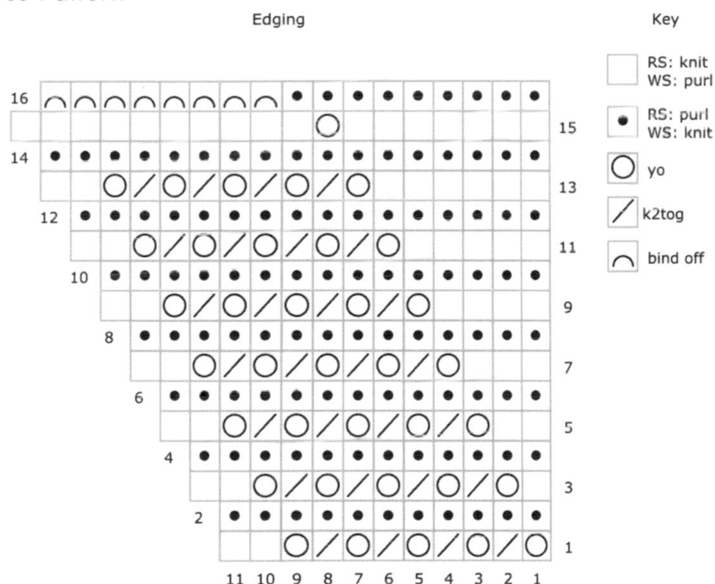

CANDY BAG

By Cécile Balladino

Worked in a gorgeous variegated yarn, this crocheted bag is the perfect thing to whip up on your travels to help carry all your new treasures. Worked in individual granny squares, this project is perfect for on the go crafting.

Materials:
Hjertegarn Kunstgarn, 1 ball in Neon 20 (MC)
Fingering weight; 420 m per 100 g ball; 75% superwash wool, 25% nylon,
Ficolana Arwetta Classic, 1 ball in Dark Olive 148 (CC)
Fingering weight; 210 m per 50 g ball; 80% Merino wool, 20% nylon

Hook

Crochet hook 3.5 mm

Gauge

Gauge is not critical for this project, just aim for a neat finish. As a guide, the squares in the sample are approximately 9 cm across.

Finished size

Approximately 38 cm wide by 24 cm deep, excluding handles.

Foundation:
Using MC, ch6 and join with a ss to form a ring.
Rnd 1: Ch3 (counts as 1tr), 2tr into ring, ch3, (3tr in ring, ch3) 3 times, join to 3rd st of beg ch with a ss.
Rnd 2: Ch3 (counts as 1tr), * 1tr in each tr, [2tr, ch3, 2tr] in each 3ch-sp; rep from * to end of rnd. Join to 3rd st of beg ch with a ss.
You will have 7tr on each side.
Rnd 3: Repeat Rnd 2.
You will have 11tr on each side.
Rnd 4: Repeat Rnd 2.
You will have 15tr on each side.
Rnd 5: Repeat Rnd 2.
You will have 19tr on each side.
Break yarn, fasten off and weave in ends.

Joining the squares
Using CC, join the squares with a row of dc. You will have to make 6 strips of 6 squares, then join these 6 strips to make a big block - see diagram.

The mouth
Foundation: Using CC, crochet 37dc evenly along one side of the block.

Change to MC.

Note: To obtain the multi-coloured effect, cut the yarn after each row and start the next row by taking the yarn from the other end of the ball.
Row 1 : Ch1 (does not count as st), 1dc in st at base of ch, *ch1, skip 1 st, 1dc in next st; rep from * to end, turn.
Row 2: Ch2 (counts as 1dc, ch1), 1dc in the next 1ch-sp, *ch1, 1dc in the next 1ch-sp; rep from * to last st, 1dc in last st, turn.

Rep Row 2 until you have 11 rows in total.

Row 12: Change to CC and rep Row 2. Break yarn and fasten off, leaving a long tail.
Fold this strip in two and sew along underside edge of block using invisible stitches.
Rep on the opposite side of the block.

The handles
Foundation: Using CC, crochet 45dc evenly along one unfinished side of the block, ch99, 45dc along the opposite unfinished side of the block, ch99, join to first dc with a ss. Break yarn and fasten off.

Note: To obtain the multi-coloured effect, cut the yarn after each rnd and start the next rnd by taking the yarn from the other end of the ball.

Change to MC.
Rnd 1: Ch1 (does not count as st), 1dc in each st around, join to first dc with a ss.
Rnd 2: Ch1 (does not count as st, 1dc in st at base of ch, ch1, miss 1 st, * 1dc in next st, ch1, miss 1 st; rep from * to end, join to first dc with a ss.
Rnd 3: Ss into first 1ch-sp, ch2 (counts as 1dc, ch1), * 1dc in the next 1ch-sp, ch1; rep from * to end, join to first ch1 with a ss.

Rep Rnd 3 until you have 15 rnds.

Do one last repeat of Rnd 3 with CC yarn. Break yarn and fasten off.

Finishing
Sew the edge of the mouth strip to the edge of the handle with invisible stitches.
Fold the handle in two and close with a row of slip stitches all around. Weave in ends.

Now, enjoy your bag!

GOING UNDERGROUND BAG

By Jacqui Harding

This bag was made with practicality in mind. Perfect for travelling light around London, it's big enough to hold event tickets and other essentials, and has an internal pocket that's ideal for your Oyster card.

There's even a matching mini-purse so you can carry the cash you need without the bulk of your everyday purse. The wrist strap means you can be sure that the contents are secure, and that you don't have to clutch your bag all night. Using only small amounts of precious fabric, you can play with colour and print to your heart's content. If you are also a hooker, why not crochet your own rickrack style trim. As it's a small project, it is possible to hand sew this bag. You do need to use interfacing, whether fusible or not, in order to keep the structure of the bag and to keep it looking good for years to come.

Materials:

2x fat quarters of fabrics. You could use 3 smaller pieces if you want a contrasting lining. Sample shown was made with 3 fat quarters of Liberty of London Tana Lawn cotton.

Medium weight fusible interfacing – small amount needed, approximately one quarter metre.

Approximately 21 x 30 cm curtain interlining. I like this because it is cheap and easily available. You could also use fusible fleece or light wadding

Bag

Other supplies

1 x 20 cm plastic zip for bag, 1 x 12 cm plastic zip for purse – I generally buy longer zips and cut to size
Optional trim – crochet rickrack, ribbon, lace trim, covered piping cord.
Optional: Spray starch for easy ironing.
For crochet trim: 2 x 8 m hanks embroidery thread. 3.25 mm hook.

Finished size

Bag: 29.5 cm at widest point, 16cm high, 13cm handle, 20 cm at top
Purse: 14.5 cm at widest point, 8.5 cm high, 11 cm opening

All seam allowances 1 cm

Preparation

Print out pattern sheet (found on page 141), adjusting size to 100% scale on borderless A4. Check that pattern pieces are correct size by measuring the width of the small purse at the widest point – this measurement should be 16.5 cm. Cut out pieces as per pattern sheet. Cut the interlining pieces smaller by approximately 1 cm all around. Iron all fabric pieces. Attach all fusible interfacing pieces to the external fabrics apart from the main body. For the bag body, with WS facing, centre the interlining on the fabric, then put the fusible interfacing with glue side down onto the fabric. There should be a space all around the interlining for the fusible interfacing to stick to the fabric.

Handle

Make handle – iron the rectangle of fabric in half lengthwise, WST. Open out, and press each side in towards the centre line. Fold in half (4 layers thick) and topstitch close to each edge. Put aside.

Abbreviations:

RST	Right sides together
WST	Wrong sides together
Ext	Exterior

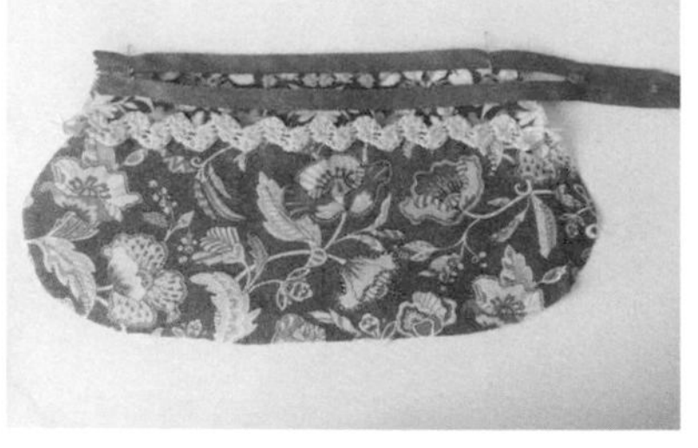

Exterior
Place bag body and top RST. If you are using piping or lace, sandwich it between the layers. Sew with 1cm seam allowance. Press towards body of bag. Attach crochet trim or ribbon to RS over seam, or edge stitch to keep in place. Repeat for other side.

Interior
Make the pocket. Fold pocket piece in half RST and sew around, leaving a 5cm gap unsewn. Clip corners, turn out & press. Topstitch along top edge, then pin pocket in position on lining bag body. Sew carefully around side and bottom edges of the pocket, making sure to secure opening as you sew.

Repeat step 2 above.
Attach zip:
Following the procedure in the pictures below, attach zip. First sew onto ext fabric, then sandwich the zip between ext & lining fabrics, sew along previous line. Repeat for other side. Excess zip can be cut off later.

Ensure you open the zip half way before sewing the last step!

Check that the construction is ok & there are no gaps/wonky seams by turning the bag RS out by pulling it through the gap in the lining. If it all looks ok, turn the bag inside out to neaten & finish by cutting notches in curved seams & cutting off any excess zip. Pull bag through gap again. Use a chop stick/crochet hook to fully open out seams, check all seams look ok then sew closed the gap in the lining. Push the lining into the bag and press to finish.

Crochet rickrack trim:
Written using UK crochet terms.
Ch3, 5tr into 1st ch, turn. *Ch2, 5tr into 2nd tr from hook, turn. Rep from * until your trim is long enough to fit your bag.
This trim is very stretchy. I used 1 hank of embroidery thread per side, but feel free to use some souvenir yarn instead!

Purse
The purse is a simpler version of the bag, without the top section, trim & handle. Attach the zip as shown for the main bag, then match the fabrics with RS Exteriors & RS linings touching. Remembering to open the zip, sew around the purse leaving a gap in the lining. Clip curved seams, cut off excess zip. Pull bag through opening, open out all seams, sew gap closed. Push lining into purse & press.

KNIGHTSBRIDGE SHAWL

By Anniken Allis

This intricate lace shawl is worked from the back of the neck downward, accented with beads (or not, as you prefer). The increases form a central lace panel flanked by stockinette, and it finishes in a wide border. This is the perfect project for a very special skein of lace weight that you couldn't resist, and will fill up plenty of travel time!

Materials:
SweetGeorgia Yarns Merino Silk Lace, 1 skein in Mink lace weight; 700 m per 100 g; 50% fine Merino wool, 50% silk

Needles
3.5 mm circular needles, 80 cm

Gauge
19 sts x 23.5 rows = 10cm measured over Chart B

Pattern notes
Slip markers as you reach them unless otherwise indicated.
All the charts except for Chart C show RS rows only.

Sizing
Wingspan: 176 cm
Depth (centre back): 76 cm

Other supplies
Approximately 135 size 8 seed beads.
Sample shown used Debbie Abrahams Beads, Shade 608, 1 bag
0.50 mm crochet hook
stitch marker

Chart A

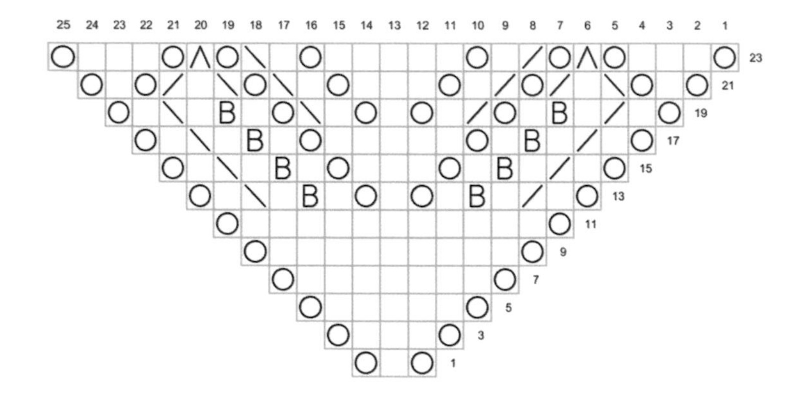

Row 1 (RS): Yo, k1, yo.
Row 2 and all WS rows: Purl.
Row 3: Yo, k3, yo
Row 5: Yo, k5, yo.
Row 7: Yo, k7, yo.
Row 9: Yo, k9, yo.
Row 11: Yo, k11, yo.
Row 13: Yo, k1, k2tog, k1, B, [k1, yo] twice, k1, B, k1, ssk, k1, yo.
Row 15: Yo, k1, k2tog, k1, B, k1, yo, k3, yo, k1, B, k1, ssk, k1, yo.
Row 17: Yo, k1, k2tog, k1, B, k1, yo, k5, yo, k1, B, k1, ssk, k1, yo.
Row 19: Yo, k1, k2tog, k1, B, k1, yo, k2tog, [k1, yo] twice, k1, ssk, yo, k1, B, k1, ssk, k1, yo.
Row 21: Yo, k1, yo, ssk, k1, k2tog, yo, k2tog, k1, yo, k3, yo, k1, ssk, yo, ssk, k1, k2tog, yo, k1, yo.
Row 23: Yo, k3, yo, sk2p, yo, k2tog, k1, yo, k5, yo, k1, ssk, yo, sk2p, yo, k3, yo.

Chart B

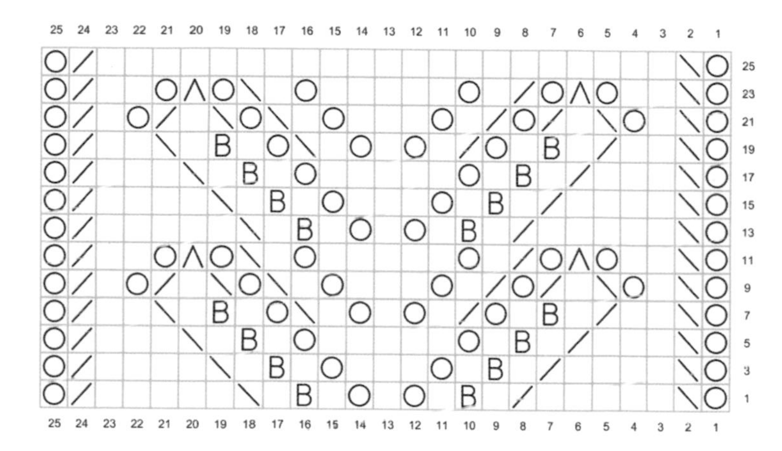

Row 1 (RS): Yo, ssk, k5, k2tog, k1, B, [k1, yo] twice, k1, B, k1, ssk, k5, k2tog, yo.
Row 2 and all WS rows: Purl.
Row 3: Yo, ssk, k4, k2tog, k1, B, k1, yo, k3, yo, k1, B, k1, ssk, k4, k2tog, yo.
Row 5: Yo, ssk, k3, k2tog, k1, B, k1, yo, k5, yo, k1, B, k1, ssk, k3, k2tog, yo.
Row 7: Yo, ssk, k2, k2tog, k1, B, k1, yo, k2tog, [k1, yo] twice, k1, ssk, yo, k1, B, k1, ssk, k2, k2tog, yo.
Row 9: [Yo, ssk, k1] twice, k2tog, yo, k2tog, k1, yo, k3, yo, k1, ssk, yo, ssk, [k1, k2tog, yo] twice.
Row 11: Yo, ssk, k2, yo, sk2p, yo, k2tog, k1, yo, k5, yo, k1, ssk, yo, sk2p, yo, k2, k2tog, yo.
Row 13: Yo, ssk, k5, k2tog, k1, B, [k1, yo] twice, k1, B, k1, ssk, k5, k2tog, yo.
Row 15: Yo, ssk, k4, k2tog, k1, B, k1, yo, k3, yo, k1, B, k1, ssk, k4, k2tog, yo.
Row 17: Yo, ssk, k3, k2tog, k1, B, k1, yo, k5, yo, k1, B, k1, ssk, k3, k2tog, yo.
Row 19: Yo, ssk, k2, k2tog, k1, B, k1, yo, k2tog, [k1, yo] twice, k1, ssk, yo, k1, B, k1, ssk, k2, k2tog, yo.
Row 21: [Yo, ssk, k1] twice, k2tog, yo, k2tog, k1, yo, k3, yo, k1, ssk, yo, ssk, [k1, k2tog, yo] twice.
Row 23: Yo, ssk, k2, yo, sk2p, yo, k2tog, k1, yo, k5, yo, k1, ssk, yo, sk2p, yo, k2, k2tog, yo.
Row 25: Yo, ssk, k21, k2tog, yo.

Chart C

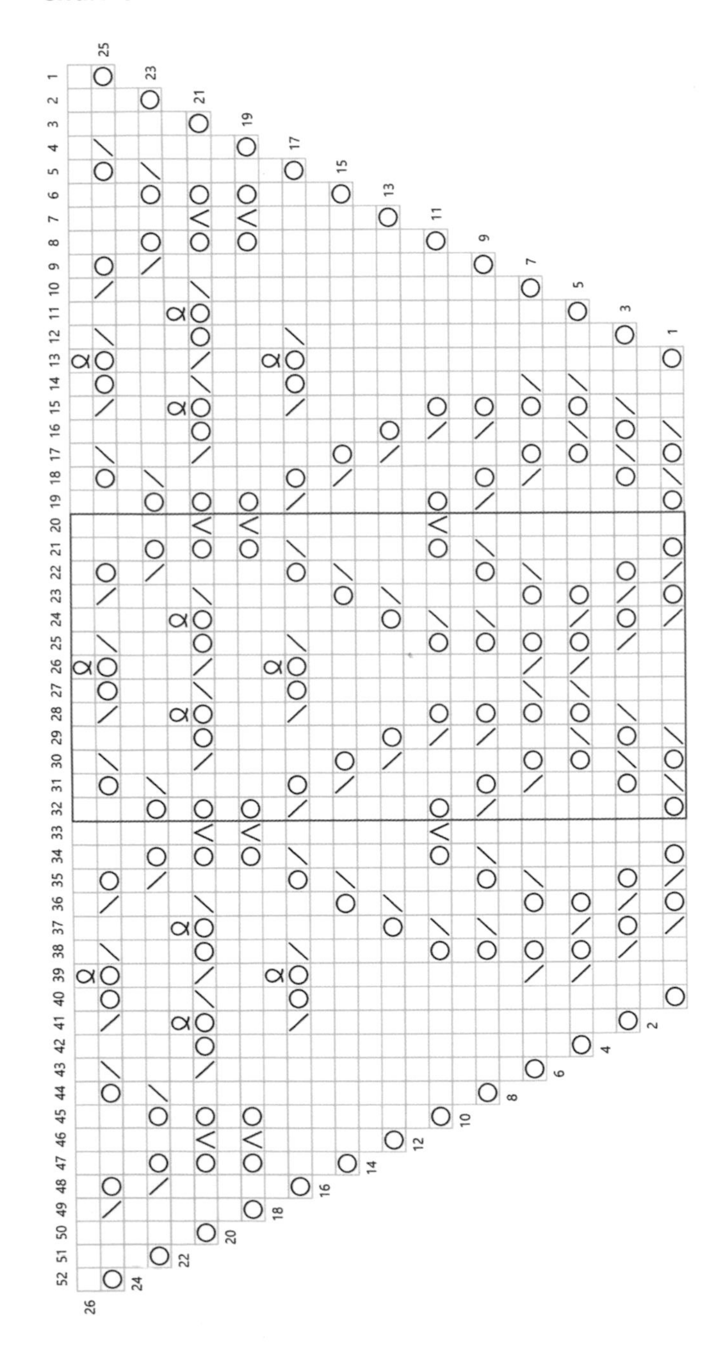

1 2 3 4 5 6 7 8 9 10 11 12 13 14 15 16 17 18 19 20 21 22 23 24 25 26 27 28 29 30 31 32 33 34 35 36 37 38 39 40 41 42 43 44 45 46 47 48 49 50 51 52
25 23 21 19 17 15 13 11 9 7 5 3 1
2 4 6 8 10 12 14 16 18 20 22 24 26

Please note: stitch pattern repeat is indicated by square brackets.

Row 1 (RS): Yo, k2, [k2tog, yo] twice, [k1, (yo, ssk) twice, k4, (k2tog, yo) twice], k1, [yo, ssk] twice, k2, yo.
Row 2 (WS): Purl.
Row 3: Yo, k2, [k2tog, yo] twice, k1, [k2, (yo, ssk) twice, k2, (k2tog, yo) twice, k1], k2, [yo, ssk] twice, k2, yo.
Row 4: Purl.
Row 5: Yo, k2, [k2tog, yo] twice, k2, [k3, (yo, ssk) twice, (k2tog, yo) twice, k2], k3, [yo, ssk] twice, k2, yo.
Row 6: Purl.
Row 7: Yo, k3, k2tog, yo, k1, yo, ssk, k1, [k2, (k2tog, yo, k1, yo, ssk) twice, k1], k2, k2tog, yo, k1, yo, ssk, k3, yo.
Row 8: Purl.
Row 9: Yo, k5, yo, ssk, k1, yo, ssk, [(k1, k2tog, yo) twice, k2, yo, ssk, k1, yo, ssk], [k1, k2tog, yo] twice, k5, yo.
Row 10: Purl.
Row 11: Yo, k6, yo, ssk, k2, yo, [sk2p, yo, k2, k2tog, yo, k2, yo, ssk, k2, yo], sk2p, yo, k2, k2tog, yo, k6, yo.
Row 12: Purl.
Row 13: Yo, k8, yo, ssk, k2, [k3, k2tog, yo, k4, yo, ssk, k2], k3, k2tog, yo, k8, yo.
Row 14: Purl.
Row 15: Yo, k10, yo, ssk, k1, [k2, k2tog, yo, k6, yo, ssk, k1], k2, k2tog, yo, k10, yo.
Row 16: Purl.
Row 17: Yo, k6, k2tog, yo twice, ssk, k2, yo, ssk, [k1, k2tog, yo, k2, k2tog, yo twice, ssk, k2, yo, ssk], k1, k2tog, yo, k2, k2tog, yo twice, ssk, k6, yo.
Row 18: P9, p tbl, p6, [p6, p tbl, p6], p6, p tbl, p8.
Row 19: Yo, k1, yo, sk2p, yo, k10, yo, [sk2p, yo, k10, yo], sk2p, yo, k10, yo, sk2p, yo, k1, yo.
Row 20: Purl.
Row 21: Yo, k2, yo, sk2p, yo, k1, [k2tog, yo twice, ssk] twice, k1, yo, [sk2p, yo, k1, (k2tog, yo twice, ssk) twice, k1, yo], sk2p, yo, k1, (k2tog, yo twice, ssk) twice, k1, yo, sk2p, yo, k2, yo.
Row 22: P9, p tbl, p3, p tbl, p4, [p4, p tbl, p3, p tbl, p4], p4, p tbl, p3, p tbl, p8.
Row 23: Yo, k2, k2tog, yo, k1, yo, ssk, k8, k2tog, yo, [k1, yo, ssk, k8, k2tog, yo], k1, yo, ssk, k8, k2tog, yo, k1, yo, ssk, k2, yo.
Row 24: Purl.
Row 25: Yo, k2, k2tog, yo, k3, yo, ssk, k1, k2tog, yo twice, ssk, k1, k2tog, yo, k1, [k2, yo, ssk, k1, k2tog, yo twice, ssk, k1, k2tog, yo, k1], k2, yo, ssk, k1, k2tog, yo twice, ssk, k1, k2tog, yo, k3, yo, ssk, k2, yo.
Row 26: P13, p tbl, p6, [p6, p tbl, p6], p6, p tbl, p12.

Chart D

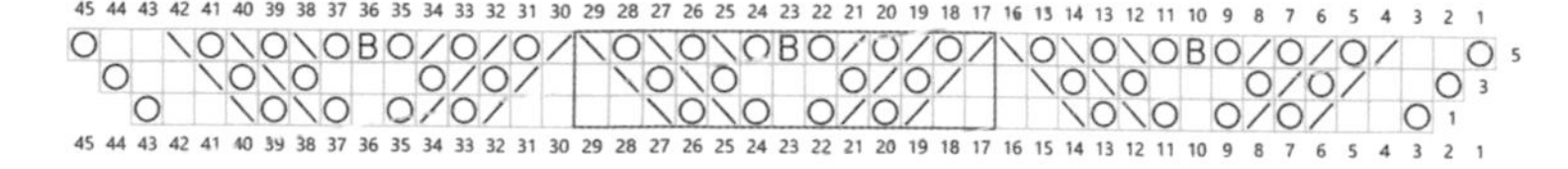

Row 1 (RS): Yo, k2, [k2tog, yo] twice, k1, [yo, ssk] twice, k2, [k2, (k2tog, yo) twice, k1, (yo, ssk) twice, k2], k2, [k2tog, yo] twice, k1, [yo, ssk] twice, k2, yo.
Row 2 and all WS rows: Purl.
Row 3: Yo, k2, [k2tog, yo] twice, k3, [yo, ssk] twice, k1, [k1, (k2tog, yo) twice, k3, (yo, ssk) twice, k1], k1, [k2tog, yo] twice, k3, [yo, ssk] twice, k2, yo.
Row 5: Yo, k2, [k2tog, yo] three times, B, [yo, ssk] three times, [(k2tog, yo) three times, B, (yo, ssk) three times], [k2tog, yo] three times, B, [yo, ssk] three times, k2, yo.

Chart E

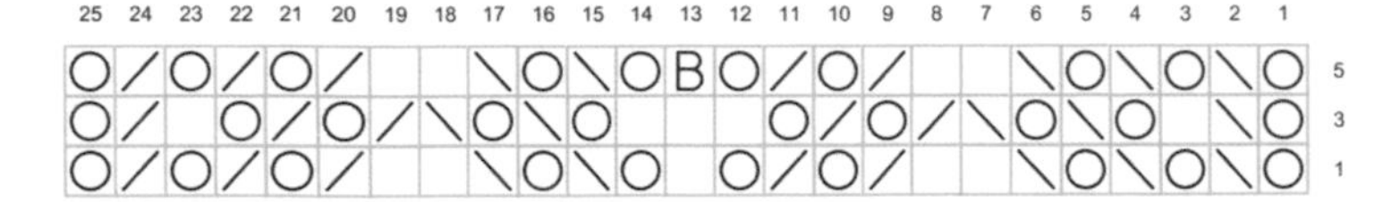

Row 1 (RS): [Yo, ssk] three times, k2, [k2tog, yo] twice, k1, [yo, ssk] twice, k2, [k2tog, yo] three times.
Row 2 and all WS rows: Purl.
Row 3: Yo, ssk, k1, [yo, ssk] twice, [k2tog, yo] twice, k3, [yo, ssk] twice, [k2tog, yo] twice, k1, k2tog, yo.

Row 5: [yo, ssk] three times, k2, [k2tog, yo] twice, B, [yo, ssk] twice, k2, [k2tog, yo] three times.

Pattern
Cast on 11 sts. Knit one row.

Begin Chart A:
Row 1 (RS): Sl1 wyif, k1, yo, k2, yo,pm, k1, work Row 1 of Chart A,pm, k1, yo, k2, yo, k2 - 17 sts.
Row 2 and all WS rows unless otherwise stated: Sl1 wyif, k1, p to last 2 sts, k2.
Row 3: Sl1 wyif, k1, yo, k4, yo, k1, work Row 3 of Chart A, k1, yo, k4, yo, k2 - 23 sts.
Row 5: Sl1 wyif, k1, yo, k6, yo, k1, work Row 5 of Chart A, k1, yo, k6, yo, k2 - 29 sts.
Row 7: Sl1 wyif, k1, yo, k to marker, yo, k1, work Row 7 of Chart A, k1, yo, k to last 2 sts, yo, k2 - 33 sts.

Continue as established, working all 24 rows of Chart A once - 83 sts.

Begin Chart B:
Row 1 (RS): Sl1 wyif, k1, k to marker, yo, k1, work Row 1 of Chart B, k1, yo, k to last 2 sts, yo, k2 - 4 sts inc.
Row 3: Sl1 wyif, k1, k to marker, yo, k1, work Row 3 of Chart B, k1, yo, k to last 2 sts, yo, k2 - 4 sts inc.

Continue working until all 26 rows of Chart B worked twice - 187 sts.

Begin Chart C:
Row 1 (RS): Sl1 wyif, k1, work Row 1 of Chart C working the 13 st patt rep 5 times, k1, work Row 1 of Chart B, k1, work Row 1 of Chart C working the 13 st patt rep 5 times, k2 - 4 sts inc.
Row 2 and all WS rows: Sl1 wyif, k1, work Row 2 of Chart C working the 13 st patt rep 5 times, p1, p25, p1, work Row 2 of Chart C working the 13 st patt rep 5 times, k2 - 4 sts inc.

Continue working until all 26 rows of Chart C and Chart B are worked 4 times - 395 sts.

Begin Charts D and E
Row 1: Sl1 wyif, k1, work Row 1 of Chart D working the 13 st patt rep 12 times, k1, work Row 1 of Chart E, k1, work Row 1 of Chart D working the 13 st patt rep 12 times, k2 - 4 sts inc.
Row 2 and all WS rows: Sl1 wyif, k1, p to last 2 sts, k2.
Row 3: Sl1 wyif, k1, work Row 3 of Chart D working the 13 st patt rep 12 times, k1, work Row 1 of Chart E, k1, work Row 3 of Chart D working the 13 st patt rep 12 times, k2 - 4 sts inc.

Continue working until all 6 rows of Chart D and Chart E are worked once - 407 sts.

Using a stretchy cast off, cast off all sts.

Finishing
Weave in ends and block shawl to given measurements.

KNITTER'S TOOL ROLL

By Catherine Hopkins

Knitters can be sewists too...and what better marriage of the two crafts then a tool roll that contains everything you could possible want for projects on the go! There's measuring tapes, a place for needles and thread, and storage for scissors, needles and hooks. You can make this up before you leave on your trip, or find some luscious fabrics on your holiday to make a special tool roll when you get home.

Materials:

80 cm of cotton fabric (120 cm width) or one fat quarter plus scraps
20c m zip fastener
small piece of knitting (a tension square/small gauge swatch is ideal)
2 m of petersham ribbon one marked out in inches, one centimetres
2.5 m cotton trim (lace, rickrack or similar)
piece of fusible interlining 50 x 23 cm
cotton thread

Preparation
Cut out the following shapes from the cotton fabric (all measurements are incm)

A) 50 x 23 – cut two (for the main body)
B) 23 x 20 (zip pocket)
C) 22 x 22 (gauge pocket)
D) 20 x 23 – cut two (crochet hook, DPN slots and flap)
E) 103 x 16 - straight strip (tape measure)
F) 4 x 30 - bias strip (scissor holder)

Construction
1. Round off the corners of the two main body pieces (A) and the zip pocket (B) – see Figure 1. You can use a small cup or similar object to get the shape or cut freehand. The idea is that a gentle curve will be easier to stitch around when adding the trim.

2. Iron the interfacing onto the wrong side of one piece A.

3. Fold piece B in half so that it is 23 x 10cm and press.

4. On the wrong side of the zip fastener, align the fold of piece B a little way away from the teeth of the zip and stitch (Figure 2).

5. Turn piece B over and pin to the right side of the interfaced piece A. Stitch upper section of zip fastener tape to piece A (the whole of the zip will be visible and piece B will cover roughly one third of piece A – Figure 3).

6. Fold piece F in half lengthwise with the wrong sides together and sew a 1 cm seam. Turn right side out.

7. Fold piece C in half with the wrong sides together and sew a 1 cm seam down the long side, opposite the fold. Press the seam open and turn half of the tube to the right side, so that you will have a shallow tube with the right side of the fabric inside and out. Press flat with the seam running down the centre of one side.

8. Fold piece E in half with the right sides together and press. Open out. Using the fold as a guide, sew one piece of the petersham ribbon down the length of the tape, 1 cm from the fold. It is important to place the 0 position of the tape 1 cm away from the raw edges of one short edge. Stitch down both sides of the tape.

10. Leaving a 1-2 cm gap after piece B, place the knitted swatch to the left 2 cm below the upper raw edge. Pin and sew into place.

11. Fold piece F in half to form a large loop, and tack it to the middle of the back of piece C, matching the raw edges and using the seam line as a position marker. Pin piece C to the lower edge of the main body piece, below the
knitted swatch.

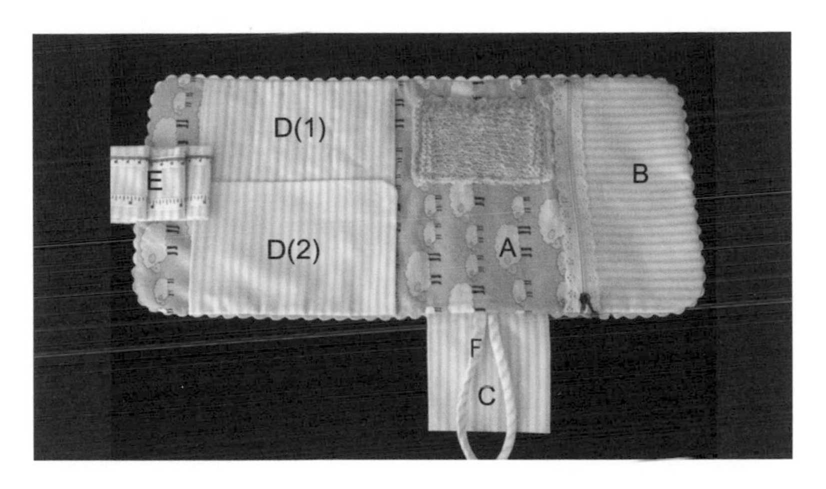

12. Line up the pocket section of piece D with the upper raw edge, raw edges together, turn under 1cm on the right hand side edge and sew in place.

13. Keeping the pocket piece D flat, mark where you want to position the pockets (the width will depend on the size and number of crochet hooks, DPNs, etc. you want to keep in the roll). Place a pin at each mark. Turn under 1 cm at the left hand edge. Stitch down the left hand edge and work lines of machine stitching to form the individual pockets.

14. Position the flap from the second piece D directly below the pockets and pin into place.

15. Pin the remaining raw edge of the measuring tape, piece E, to the centre of the left hand edge and pin into place.

16. Pin your chosen trim around the main body piece along the 1cm seam line, over all the pocket placements. Remember to have the decorative edge pointing inwards at this point.

17. Place the second main body piece A on top, right sides down so that all the pockets and trim are sandwiched in the middle. Stitch a 1cm seam all around, leaving about 10cm along the pocket flap (piece D) open for turning right side out

18. Trim, clip curves and turn right side out. Hand or machine stitch the open section and press.

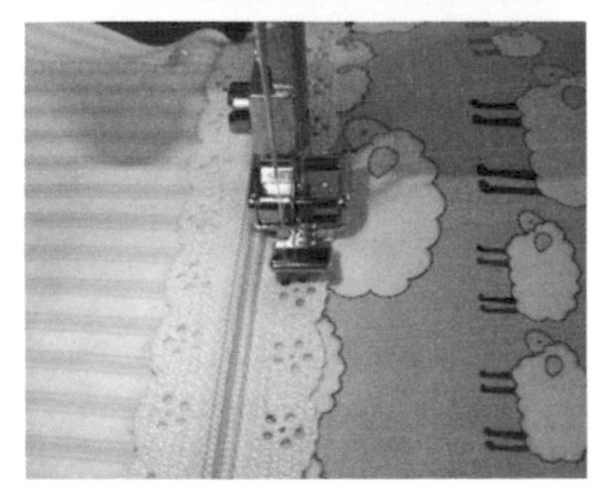

LA VILLE DE L'AMOUR

By Fiona Hamilton-MacLaren

Ah Paris...what city is more romantic, more inspiring or more worthy of being immortalised in a fabulous pair of socks? Inspired by the romance of Paris and every knitter's love of yarn, these socks incorporate lace stitches and cables to create an Eiffel Tower pattern with cupped hearts blooming out of twisted stitches on the outside of the leg. They are worked from the toe up with a short row heel.

Materials:

Travelknitter BFL Supersock, 1 skein in Puddled Iron.

Fingering weight; 425 m per 100 g; 75% wool, 25% nylon

Socks

Needles

2.25 mm, either double pointed needles or circulars for working in the round.

Gauge

36 sts x 48 rnds = 10 cm in stocking stitch (unstretched)

Other supplies

cable needle
stitch markers
tapestry needle

Sizing

XS (S, M, L, XL), to fit 15.5 (18, 20.5, 23, 25.5) cm foot circumference.
Actual foot circumference: 14.5 (16, 17.75, 19.5, 20) cm

Special Stitches

Four stitch cable (C4): Slip 2 sts to cable needle; for right sock, hold to the back of work, for left sock, hold to the front of work. Knit next 2 sts, knit 2 sts from cable needle.
Left twist (LT): Slip 2 sts knitwise, one at a time. Return these sts to the left needle, and knit the second st through back loop, leaving it on the needle. K2tog through back loop, and drop both sts off the needle.
1/1 Left purl cable (1/1 LPC): Slip one st to cable needle, hold to front of work. Purl next st, knit st from cable needle.
1/1 Right purl cable (1/1 RPC): Slip one st to cable needle, hold to back of work. Knit next st, purl st from cable needle.
2/1 Left purl cable (2/1 LPC): Slip two sts to cable needle, hold to front of work. Purl next st, knit two sts from cable needle.
2/1 Right purl cable (2/1 RPC): Slip one st to cable needle, hold to back of work. Knit next two sts, purl st from cable needle.
Right twist (RT): Knit the next two sts together, leave sts on left needle. Knit the first st again, and drop both sts off the needle.

Eiffel Tower Pattern

•	•	•	•		•	13
•	•	•	•		•	
•	•	•	•		•	11
•	•	•	•		•	
•	•	•	•		•	9
•	•	•	p2tog	o	•	
•		•	•	•	•	7
•		•	•	•	•	
•		•	•	•	•	5
•		•	•	•	•	
•		•	•	•	•	3
p2tog	o	•	•	•	•	
•	•	•	•	•	•	1

☐ k
• p
o yo
p2tog
— Repeat

Eiffel Tower Pattern

Pattern repeat is Rnds 2-13 inclusive.
Rnd 1: Purl all sts.
Rnd 2: P4, yo, p2tog.
Rnds 3-7: P4, k1, p1.
Rnd 8: P1, yo, p2tog, p3.
Rnds 9-13: P1, k1, p4.

Right Twist Cable

5
3
1

k
RT
— Repeat

Right Twist Cable
Pattern repeat is Rnds 2-5 inclusive.
Rnd 1: K4.
Rnd 2: RT, RT.
Rnd 3: K4.
Rnd 4: K1, RT, k1.
Rnd 5: K4.

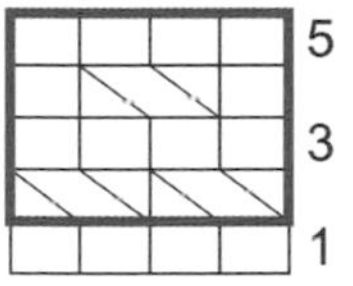

k
LT
— Repeat

Left Twist Cable
Pattern repeat is Rnds 2-5 inclusive.
Rnd 1: K4.
Rnd 2: LT, LT.
Rnd 3: K4.
Rnd 4: K1, LT, k1.
Rnd 5: K4.

Cupped Hearts Cable

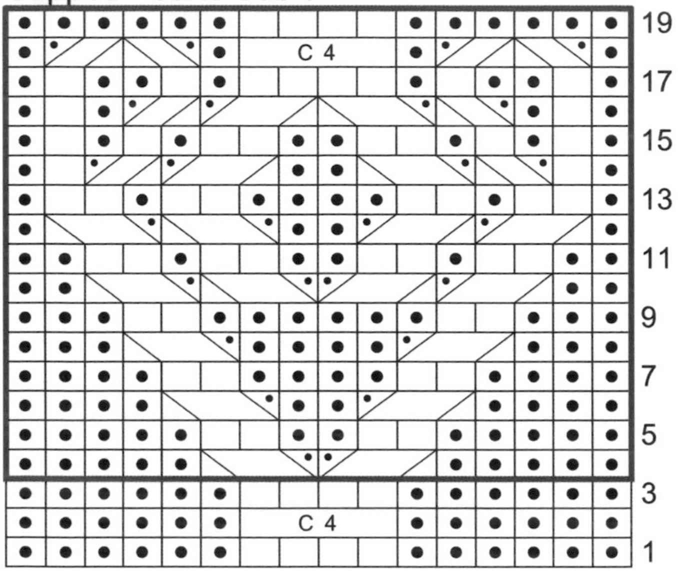

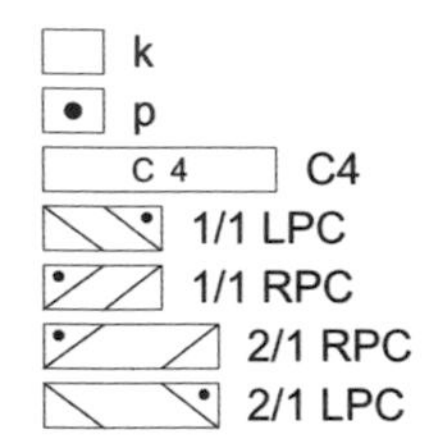

— Repeat

Cupped Hearts Cable

Pattern repeat is Rnds 4-19 inclusive.

NOTE: The direction of the cable in Rnd 2 varies with the foot being worked.

Rnd 1: P6, k4, p6.

Rnd 2: P6, C4, p6.

Rnd 3: P6, k4, p6.

Rnd 4: P5, 2/1 RPC, 2/1 LPC, p5.

Rnd 5: P5, k2, p2, k2, p5.

Rnd 6: P4, 2/1 RPC, p2, 2/1 LPC, p4.

Rnd 7: P4, k2, p4, k2, p4.

Rnd 8: P3, 2/1 RPC, p4, 2/1 LPC, p3.

Rnd 9: P3, k2, p6, k2, p3.

Rnd 10: P2, 2/1 RPC, 2/1 RPC, 2/1 LPC, 2/1 LPC, p2.

Rnd 11: P2, k2, p1, k2, p2, k2, p1, k2, p2.

Rnd 12: P1, 2/1 RPC, 2/1 RPC, p2, 2/1 LPC, 2/1 LPC, p1.

Rnd 13: P1, k2, p1, k2, p4, k2, p1, k2, p1.

Rnd 14: P1, k1, 1/1 LPC, 2/1 LPC, p2, 2/1 RPC, 1/1 RPC, k1, p1.

Rnd 15: P1, k1, p1, k1, p1, k2, p2, k2, p1, k1, p1, k1, p1.

Rnd 16: P1, k1, p1, 1/1 LPC, 2/1 LPC, 2/1 RPC, 1/1 RPC, p1, k1, p1.

Rnd 17: P1, k1, p2, k1, p1, k4, p1, k1, p2, k1, p1.

Rnd 18: P1, 1/1 LPC, 1/1 RPC, p1, C4, p1, 1/1 LPC, 1/1 RPC, p1.

Rnd 19: P6, k4, p6.

Pattern notes

The top of the foot is worked in pattern; the sole is worked in St st. The start of the round is positioned differently for the left and right foot to ensure the heart cable is on the outside of both feet.

The short row heel is worked flat. The unused stitches can be stored on a spare circular needle or DPN(s) while you work the heel.

The leg is worked in the Eiffel tower lace pattern with the twisted stitch cable opening into cupped hearts on the outside of the leg. If the heel was worked with a row other than 7 or 13, a reverse stockinette band is worked across the back of the leg until one of those rows has been worked.

Pattern

Toe and Foot

Provisionally cast on 20 (22, 24, 26, 24) sts.
Set Up Rnd: K10 (11, 12, 13, 12), pm, k10 (11, 12, 13, 12) pm.

Increase for the toe as follows:
Rnd 1: *k1, M1L, k to 1 st before marker, M1R, k1, sm; rep from * to end.
Rnd 2: Knit.

Repeat Rnds 1 and 2 until there are 52 (58, 64, 70, 72) sts.
Knit 2 (2, 3, 3, 3) rnds, removing second marker as you pass it on the final rnd.

Right foot

Rnd 1: Sm, k2 (0, 2, 0, 2) sts, work Rnd 1 of Eiffel Tower Pattern over 18 (24, 24, 30, 30) sts using charts or written instructions, work Rnd 1 of Right Twist Cable using charts or written instructions, p1, k to end.

Continue to work in pattern as established, until foot measures 17 (19, 21, 23.5, 25) cm from the cast on edge, or 4 (4, 4.5, 4.5, 5) cm less than desired length to heel. Proceed to Heel section.

Left foot

NOTE: If you want the lace pattern to mirror the right foot, work Rnd 1 of the Eiffel Tower Pattern then skip to Rnd 8. After the first repeat, continue working stitch pattern according to chart or written directions as given.

Rnd 1: Sm, k27 (29, 33, 35, 39), p1, work Left Twist Cable, work Eiffel Tower Pattern over 18 (24, 24, 30, 30) sts, k2(0, 2, 0, 2).

Continue to work in pattern as established, using charts or written directions, until foot measures 17 (19, 21, 23.5, 25) cm from the cast on edge, or 4 (4, 4.5, 4.5, 5) cm less than desired length. Proceed to Heel section.

Heel

Right foot

Set up Row: Work first 25 (29, 31, 35, 37) sts in pattern as established, making a note of the Eiffel Tower Pattern rnd worked.
Row 1 (RS): K28 (28, 34, 34, 40) sts, w&t.
Row 2 (WS): P27 (27, 33, 33, 39), w&t.
Row 3: Knit to one st before wrapped st, w&t.
Row 4: Purl to one st before wrapped st, w&t.

Rep Rows 3 and 4 until 11 (11, 13, 13, 13) sts remain unwrapped, finishing with a WS row.
Row 5 (RS): Knit to first wrapped st, pick up wrap and knit with st, w&t.
Row 6 (WS): Purl to first wrapped st, pick up wrap and purl with st, w&t.
Row 7: Knit to next wrapped st, pick up wraps and knit with st, w&t.
Row 8: Purl to next wrapped st, pick up wraps and purl with st, w&t.

Rep Rows 7 and 8 until two double wrapped sts remain (one on either side of the heel), ending with a WS row.
Row 9: Knit to next wrapped st, pick up wraps and knit with st,pm for the beginning of the rnd.

Left foot
Row 1: K26 (28, 32, 34, 38), w&t.

Work as for right foot from Row 2 until two double wrapped stitches remain (one on either side of the heel), ending with a WS row.

Row 9: Knit to next wrapped st, pick up wraps and knit with st, work across 23 (29, 29, 35, 35) sts in pattern as established,pm for the beginning of the rnd. Make a note of the Eiffel Tower Pattern rnd just worked.

Leg
Right foot
Note: Pick up the final pair of wraps and work them with the st as you pass them on the first rnd.
If the last Eiffel Tower Pattern rnd worked was Rnd 7 or 13:
Start with Rnd 8 or 1 of the Eiffel Tower Pattern as appropriate.
Rnd 1: Sm, work Eiffel Tower Pattern over 18 (24, 24, 30, 30) sts, work Right Twist Cable, work Eiffel Tower Pattern to last 0 (0, 0, 0, 2) sts, purl to end of rnd.

Rep Rnd 1 until 6 rnds of the Eiffel Tower Pattern have been worked.

Rnd 2: Sm, work Eiffel Tower Pattern across 12 (18, 18, 24, 24) sts, work Rnd 1 of Cupped Hearts Cable, work Eiffel Tower Pattern to end of rnd.

Rep Rnd 2 until the leg, including the heel, measures 13 (14.5, 15.5, 17, 19.5) cm or approximately 2 (2.5, 2.5, 3, 3) cm less than the desired length, finishing after Rnd 18 of the Cupped Heart Cable for best effect.

If the last Eiffel Tower Pattern rnd worked was any other pattern rnd:
Start on the appropriate pattern rnd.
Rnd 1: Sm, work Eiffel Tower Pattern over 18 (24, 24, 30, 30) sts, work Right Twist Cable, purl to end of rnd.

Rep Rnd 1 until either Rnd 7 or 13 of the Eiffel Tower Pattern has been worked.

Rnd 2: Sm, work Eiffel Tower stitch pattern across 12 (18, 18, 24, 24) sts, work Rnd 1 of Cupped Hearts Cable, work Eiffel Tower Pattern to end of rnd.

Rep Rnd 2 until the leg, including the heel, measures 13 (14.5, 15.5, 17, 19.5) cm or approximately 2 (2.5, 2.5, 3, 3) cm less than the desired length, finishing after Rnd 18 of the Cupped Heart Cable for best effect.

Left foot
If the last pattern rnd worked was Rnd 7 or 13:
Start with Rnd 8 or 1 of the Eiffel Tower Pattern as appropriate.
Rnd 1: Sm, work Eiffel Tower Pattern over 30 (30, 36, 36, 36) sts, p0 (0, 0, 0, 2) sts, work Left Twist Cable, work Eiffel Tower Pattern to end of rnd.

Rep Rnd 1 until 6 rows of the Eiffel Tower Pattern have been worked.

Rnd 2: Sm, work Eiffel Tower Pattern over 24 (24, 30, 30, 30) sts, p0 (0, 0, 0, 2) sts, work Rnd 1 of Cupped Hearts Cable, work Eiffel Tower Pattern to end of rnd.

Rep Rnd 2 until the leg, including the heel, measures 13 (14.5, 15.5, 17, 19.5) cm or approximately 2 (2.5, 2.5, 3, 3) cm less than the desired length, finishing after Rnd 18 of the Cupped Heart Cable for best effect.

If the last pattern rnd worked was any other pattern rnd:
Start on the appropriate pattern rnd.
Rnd 1: Sm, p30 (30, 36, 36, 38) sts, work Left Twist Cable, work Eiffel Tower Pattern to end of rnd.

Rep Rnd 1 until either Rnd 7 or 13 of the Eiffel Tower Pattern has been worked.

Rnd 2: Sm, work Eiffel Tower Pattern over 24 (24, 30, 30, 30) sts, purl 0 (0, 0, 0, 2) sts, work Rnd 1 of Cupped Hearts Cable, work Eiffel Tower Pattern to end of rnd.

Rep Rnd 2 until the leg, including the heel, measures 13 (14.5, 15.5, 17, 19.5)cm or approximately 2 (2.5, 2.5, 3, 3) cm less than the desired length, finishing after Rnd 18 of the Cupped Heart Cable for best effect.

Ribbing
Rnd 1:*k1, p1; repeat from * to end.

Rep Rnd 1 10 (12, 12, 14, 14) times. You can adjust the length of the ribbing by working more or fewer rounds. Cast off using a loose cast off.

Finishing
Weave in ends and block as desired.
Make a second sock following the opposite foot directions.

SOUTH BANK SHAWL

By K. M. Bedigan

The South Bank of the River Thames is a popular and busy tourist destination. With the London Aquarium, the British Film Institute and the iconic London Eye stretched along the riverbank towards the Millenium Footbridge, there's always something to see; from living statues to acrobats to breakdancers and gymnasts, it's never dull or boring!

This lovely lace shawl is an ode to the London Eye, a giant Ferris wheel originally constructed for the Millenium. The tallest Ferris wheel in Europe, the Eye is a popular destination for tourists and locals, as it offers a stunning view of the city from 135 metres up. Worked in a luxurious silk-blend fingering weight yarn, this pattern includes half circle and full circle versions, with optional bead accents.

PROJECTS

Materials:

The Uncommon Thread Merino Silk Fingering,
1 (2) skeins in Breath
Fingering weight; 400 m per 100 g skein;
50% superwash Merino, 50% silk
Eden Cottage Yarns Bedale 4ply, 1 (2) skeins in Hyssop
Fingering weight; 400 m per 100 g skein; 50% baby Yak,
50% Mulberry silk

Shawl

Needles
4.0 mm circular, 80 cm (120 cm)
11 (16) stitch markers

Gauge
20 sts x 28 rows = 10 cm measured over St st

Other Supplies
132 (224) Size 6 beads (optional). The beads used in sample were silver lined transparent
Crochet hook 1.25 mm or smaller for beading

Sizing
Half circle – 115 cm x 52 cm
Full circle – 115 cm diameter

Special Stitches
Sl1k2togpsso: sl1 st as if to knit, k2tog, pass the slipped stitch over

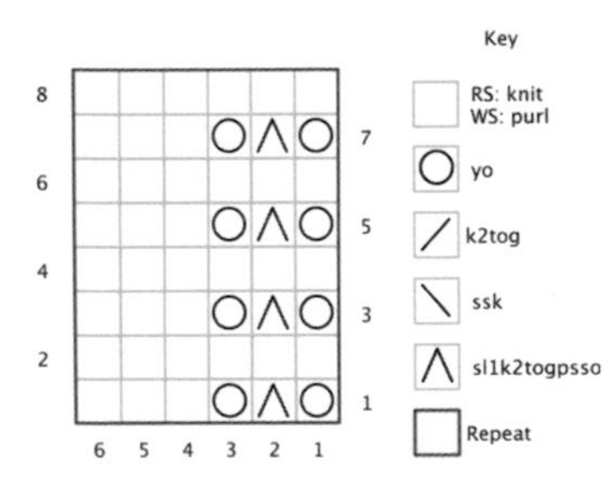

Lace Section 1
Row/Rnd 1: Yo, sl1k2togpsso, yo, k3.
Row/Rnd 2 and all even Rows (Rnd)s: Purl (knit).
Rows/Rnds 3-7: Rep Row/Rnd 1.
Row/Rnd 8: Purl (knit).

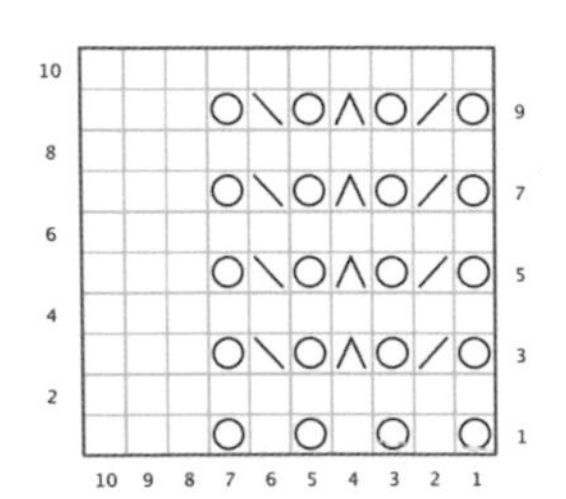

Lace Section 2
Row/Rnd 9: [Yo, k1] three times, yo, k3.
Row/Rnd 11: Yo, k2tog, yo, sl1k2togpsso, yo, ssk, yo, k3.
Rows/Rnds 13-17: Rep Row/Rnd 11.
Row/Rnd 18: Purl (knit).

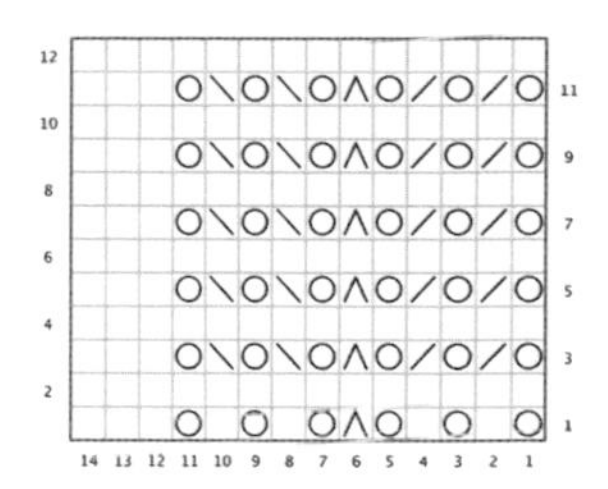

Lace Section 3

Row/Rnd 19: [Yo, k1] twice, yo, sl1k2togpsso, [yo, k1] twice, yo, k3.
Row/Rnd 21: [Yo, k2tog] twice, yo, sl1k2togpsso, [yo, ssk] twice, yo, k3.
Rows/Rnds 23-29: Rep Row/Rnd 21.
Row/Rnd 30: Purl (knit).

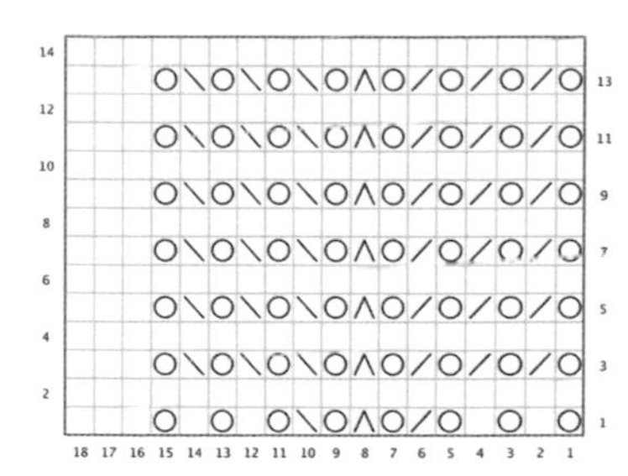

Lace Section 4

Row/Rnd 31: [Yo, k1] twice, yo, k2tog, yo, sl1k2togpsso, yo, ssk, [yo, k1] twice, yo, k3.
Row/Rnd 33: [Yo, k2tog] three times, yo, sl1k2togpsso, [yo, ssk] three times, yo, k3.
Rows/Rnds 35-43: Rep Row/Rnd 33.
Row/Rnd 44: Purl (knit).

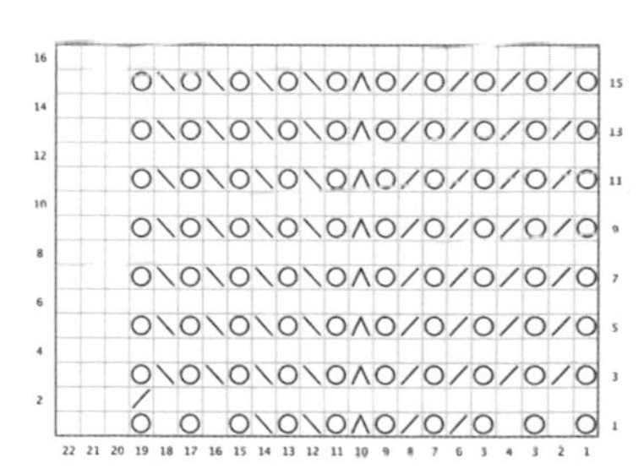

Lace Section 5

Row (Rnd) 45: [Yo, k1] twice, [yo, k2tog] twice, yo, sl1k2togpsso, [yo, ssk] twice, [yo, k1] twice, yo, k3.
Row (Rnd) 47: [Yo, k2tog] four times, yo, sl1k2togpsso, [yo, ssk] four times, yo, k3.
Rows (Rnds) 49-59: Rep Row (Rnd) 47.
Row (Rnd) 60: Purl (knit).

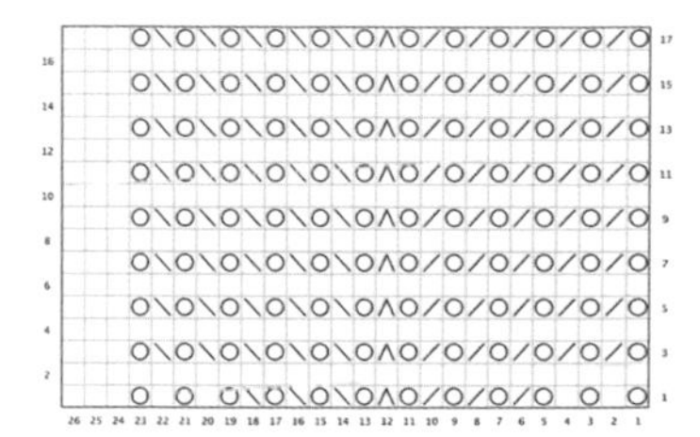

Lace Section 6

Row/Rnd 61: [Yo, k1] twice, [yo, k2tog] three times, yo, sl1k2togpsso, [yo, ssk] three times, [yo, k1] twice, yo, k3.
Row/Rnd 63: [Yo, k2tog] five times, yo, sl1k2togpsso, [yo, ssk] five times, yo, k3.
Rows/Rnds 65-77: Rep Row/Rnd 63.

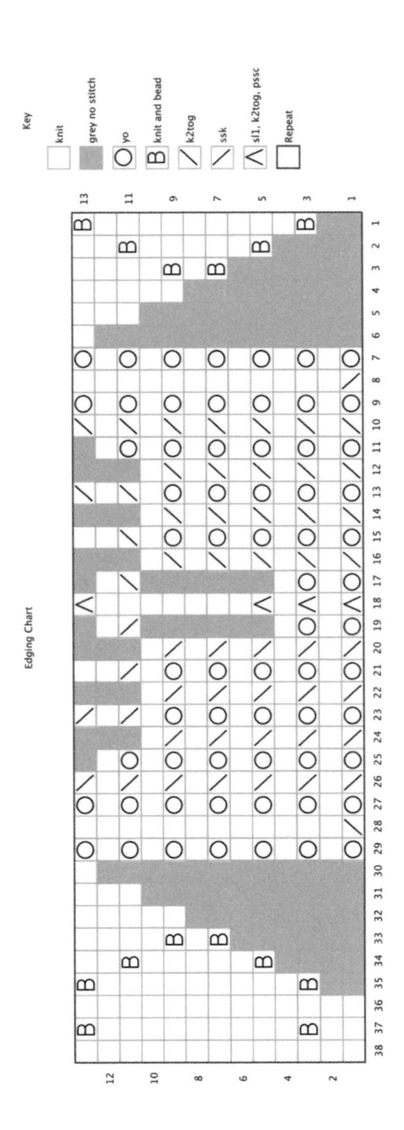

Edging

Row/Rnd 1: Yo, ssk, [yo, k2tog] four times, yo, sl1k2togpsso, [yo, ssk] four times, yo, k2tog, yo, k3.
Row/Rnd 3: B1, yo, k1, [yo, k2tog] four times, yo, sl1k2togpsso, [yo, ssk] four times, yo, k1, yo, [B1, k1] twice.
Row/Rnd 5: K1, B1, yo, k1, [yo, k2tog] four times, sl1k2togpsso, [ssk, yo] four times, k1, yo, B1, k4.
Row/Rnd 7: K2, B1, yo, k, [yo, k2tog] four times, k1, [ssk, yo] four times, k1, yo, B1, k5.
Row/Rnd 9: K2, B1, k1, yo, k1, [yo, k2tog] four times, k1, [ssk, yo] four times, k1, yo, k1, B1, k5.
Row/Rnd 11: K1, B1, k3, yo, k1, yo, k2tog, yo, k2tog three times, k1, ssk three times, yo, ssk, yo, k1, yo, k3, B1, k4.
Row/Rnd 13: B1, k5, yo, k1, yo, k2tog twice, k1, sl1k2togpsso, k1, ssk twice, yo, k1, yo, k5, [B1, k1] twice.

Half circle
Cast on 3 sts. Knit 12 rows in garter st.

Set up Row 1 (RS): K3, turn, pick up and knit 6 sts (1 per garter st ridge), turn, pick up and knit 3 sts (from cast on edge) – 12 sts.
Set up Row 2 (WS): K3,pm, p6,pm, k3.

Note: the first and last 3 sts of every row are knit, forming a garter st edging. Maintain this 3 sts edge throughout the lace patterning.

Row 1 (RS): K3, sm, [yo, k1] to marker, yo, sm, k3 – 19 sts.
Row 2: Knit.
Row 3: Knit.
Row 4: Knit.
Row 5: Knit.
Row 6: Purl.
Row 7: Knit.
Row 8: Purl.

Rep Rows 1-8 once, then Rows 7-8 once – 33 sts.
Rep Rows 1-4 once – 61 sts.

Lace Section 1
Row 1 (RS): K3, sm, yo, k2tog, yo, k3,pm, *work Row 1 of Chart 1 or Row 1 of Written Instructions, pm; rep from * to last 5 sts, yo, ssk, yo, sm, k3 – 63 sts.
Row 2 (and all WS rows until otherwise stated): K3, sm, p to last 3 sts, sm, k3.
Row 3: K3, sm, *work Row 3 of Chart 1 or Row 3 of Written Instructions, sm; rep from * to last 6 sts, yo, sl1k2togpsso, yo, sm, k3.

Work through the last row of Chart 1, or Row 8 of written directions – 63 sts.

Lace Section 2
Row 1: K3, sm, *work Row 1 of Chart 2 or Row 9 of Written Instructions, sm; rep from * to last 6 sts, [yo, k1] three times, yo, sm, k3 – 103 sts.
Row 3: K3, sm, *work Row 3 of Chart 1 or Row 11 of Written Instructions, sm; rep from * to last 10 sts, yo, k2tog, yo, sl1k2togpsso, yo, ssk,
yo, sm, k3.

Work through the last row of Chart 2, or Row 18 of Written Instructions – 103 sts.

Lace Section 3
Row 1: K3, sm, *work Row 1 of Chart 3 or Row 19 of Written Instructions, sm; rep from * to last 10 sts, [yo, k1] twice, yo, sl1k2togpsso, yo, [k1, yo] twice, sm, k3 – 143 sts.
Row 3: K3, sm, *work Row 2 of Chart 3 or Row 21 of Written Instructions, sm; rep from * to last 14 sts, [yo, k2tog] twice, yo, sl1k2togpsso, yo, [ssk, yo] twice, sm, k3.

Work through the last row of Chart 3 or Row 30 of Written Instructions – 143 sts.

Lace Section 4
Row 1: K3, sm, *work Row 1 of Chart 4 or Row 31 of Written Instructions, sm; rep from * to last 14 sts, [yo, k1] twice, yo, k2tog, yo, sl1k2togpsso, yo, ssk, yo, [k1, yo] twice, sm, k3 – 183 sts.
Row 3: K3, sm, *work Row 3 of Chart 4 or Row 33 of Written Instructions, sm; rep from * to last 18 sts, [yo, k2tog] three times, yo, sl1k2togpsso, yo, [ssk, yo] three times, sm, k3.

Work through the last row of Chart 4, or Row 44 of Written Instructions – 183 sts

Lace Section 5
Row 1: K3, sm, *work Row 1 of Chart 5 or Row 45 of Written Instructions, sm; rep from * to last 18 sts, [yo, k1] twice, [yo, k2tog] twice, yo, sl1k2togpsso, yo, [ssk, yo] twice, [k1, yo] twice, sm, k3 – 214 sts.
Row 69: K3, sm, *work Row 3 of Chart 5 or Row 47 of Written Instructions, sm; rep from * to last 22 sts, [yo, k2tog] four times, yo, sl1k2togpsso, yo, [ssk, yo] four times, sm, k3.
Work through the last row of Chart 5, or Row 60 of Written Instructions – 214 sts.

Lace Section 6
Row 1: K3, sm, *work Row 1 of Chart 6 or Row 61 of Written Instructions, sm; rep from * to last 22 sts, [yo, k1] twice, [yo, k2tog] three times, yo, sl1k2togpsso, yo, [ssk, yo] three times, [k1, yo] twice, sm, k3 – 263 sts.
Row 3: K3, sm, *work Row 3 of Chart 6 or Row 63 of Written Instructions, sm; rep from * to last 26 sts, [yo, k2tog] five times, yo, sl1k2togpsso, yo, [ssk, yo] five times, sm, k3.

Work through the last row of Chart 6, or Row 77 of Written Instructions – 263 sts.
Work 3 rows in garter st, beginning with a WS row.

Edging
Work edging from Edging Chart or Written Instructions, ending with Row 13 (RS).

Next row (WS): Knit.
Cast off as follows: K1, *slip st back onto left hand needle, k2togtbl; rep to end.

Full circle
Using your circular cast on of choice, cast on 12 sts. Join to work in the rnd, being careful not to twist.pm to mark beg of rnd.

Set up Rnd: k6, pm, k6.
Rnd 1: [yo, k1] to end – 24 sts.
Rnd 2: Knit.
Rnd 3: Knit.
Rnd 4: Knit.
Rnd 5: Knit.
Rnd 6: Purl.
Rnd 7: Knit.
Rnd 8: Purl.
Rep Rnds 1-8 once, then Rnds 7-8 once – 48 sts.
Rep Rnds 1-4 once – 96 sts.

Begin working Lace Pattern as follows:

Lace Section 1
Rnd 1: *Work Rnd 1 of Chart 1 or Rnd 1 of Written Instructions,pm; rep from * to end – 96 sts.
Rnd 2 (and all even rows unless otherwise stated): Knit.
Rnd 3: *Work Rnd 3 of Chart 1 or Rnd 3 of Written Instructions, sm; rep from * end.

Work through the last rnd of Chart 1, or Rnd 8 of Written Instructions – 96 sts.

Lace Section 2
Rnd 1: *Work Rnd 1 of Chart 2 or Rnd 9 of Written Instructions, sm; rep from * to end – 160 sts.
Rnd 3: *Work Rnd 3 of Chart 1 or Rnd 11 of Written Instructions, sm; rep from * to end.

Work through the last rnd of Chart 2, or Rnd 18 of Written Instructions – 160 sts.

Lace Section 3
Rnd 1: *Work Rnd 1 of Chart 3 or Rnd 19 of Written Instructions, sm; rep from * to end – 224 sts.
Rnd 3: *Work Rnd 3 of Chart 3 or Rnd 21 of Written Instructions, sm; rep from * to end.

Work through the last rnd of Chart 3 or Rnd 30 of Written Instructions – 224 sts.

Lace Section 4
Rnd 1: *Work Rnd 1 of Chart 4 or Rnd 31 of Written Instructions, sm; rep from * to end – 288 sts.
Rnd 3: *Work Rnd 3 of Chart 4 or Rnd 33 of Written Instructions, sm; rep from * to end.

Work through the last rnd of Chart 4, or Rnd 44 of Written Instructions – 288 sts.

Lace Section 5
Rnd 1: *Work Rnd 1 of Chart 5 or Rnd 45 of Written Instructions, sm; rep from * to end – 352 sts.
Rnd 3: K3, sm, *work Rnd 3 of Chart 5 or Rnd 47 of Written Instructions, sm; rep from * to end.

Work through the last rnd of Chart 5, or Rnd 60 of Written Instructions – 352 sts.

Lace Section 6
Rnd 1: *Work Rnd 1 of Chart 6 or Rnd 61 of Written Instructions, sm; rep from * to end – 416 sts.
Rnd 3: *Work Row 3 of Chart 6 or Row 63 of Written Instructions, sm; rep from * to end.

Work through the last rnd of Chart 6, or Rnd 77 of Written Instructions – 416 sts.

Work 3 rnds in garter st.

Edging
Work edging from Edging Chart or Written Instructions, ending with Row 13.

Next round: Purl.
Cast off as follows: K1, *slip st back onto left hand needle, k2togtbl; rep to end.

Finishing
Steam or wet block, pinning out to given measurements to open up the lace.

London
Select

WATERLOO MITTS

By Rachel Brown and Allison Thistlewood

These snuggly fingerless mitts tip a hat to the Union Jack with their red, white and blue colour scheme, and use a scrumptious angora blend yarn from a small company in the Orkney Islands of Scotland. These are a perfect first colourwork project, as there are large sections where only one colour is used. In addition, the colourwork instructions are presented in both charted and written formats, so you can pick which set to use. With an afterthought thumb and twisted ribbing, these mitts are the perfect travelling project.

Materials:
Orkney Angora St Magnus DK, 1 ball each of Navy (A), Ghost (B) and Prince Suitcase (C). B and C are exclusive colours to Loop.
DK weight; 199 m per 50 g ball; 50% wool, 50% angora
Shown in size small.

Mitts

Needles
3.5 mm DPNs, 7 cm long

Gauge
26 sts x 40 rounds = 10cm over St st

Other supplies
stitch marker
tapestry needle
waste yarn

Sizing
XS (S, M, L), to fit hand circumference of approximately 18 (20.5, 21.5, 23) cm.
Final length (cuff to hem): 22 (24, 26, 28) cm
Note: mitts are designed to fit with negative or zero ease.

Stitch patterns
Twisted rib:
Rnd 1: *K1 tbl, p1. Repeat from * to end.
Repeat Rnd 1 for pattern.

Colourwork transition:
Rnd 1: *K1 in B (C), k3 in A (B);
rep from * to end.
Rnd 2: *K4 in A (B); rep from * to end.
Rnd 3: *K2 in A (B), k1 in B (C), k1 in A (B);
rep from * to end.
Rnd 4: *K4 in A (B); rep from * to end.
Rnd 5: *K1 in B (C), k3 in A (B);
rep from * to end.
Rnd 6: *K4 in A (B); rep from * to end.
Rnd 7: *K1 in A (B), k1 in B (C);
rep from * to end.
Rnd 8: *K4 in A (B); rep from * to end.
Rnd 9: *K1 in B (C), k1 in A (B);
rep from * to end.
Rnd 10: *K4 in A (B); rep from * to end.
Rnd 11: *K1 in A (B), k1 in B (C);
rep from * to end.
Rnd 12: *K1 in B (C), k1 in A (B);
rep from * to end.
Rnds 13-14: Rep Rnds 11-12.
Rnd 15: *K4 in B (C); rep from * to end.
Rnd 16: *K1 in A (B), k1 in B (C);
rep from * to end.
Rnd 17: *K4 in B (C); rep from * to end.
Rnd 18: *K1 in B (C), k1 in A (B);
rep from * to end.
Rnd 19: *K4 in B (C); rep from * to end.
Rnd 20: *K1 in A (B), k3 in B (C);
rep from * to end.
Rnd 21: *K4 in B (C); rep from * to end.
Rnd 22: *K2 in B (C), k1 in A (B), k1 in B (C);
rep from * to end.
Rnd 23: *K4 in B (C); rep from * to end.
Rnd 24: *K1 in A (B), k3 in B (C);
rep from * to end

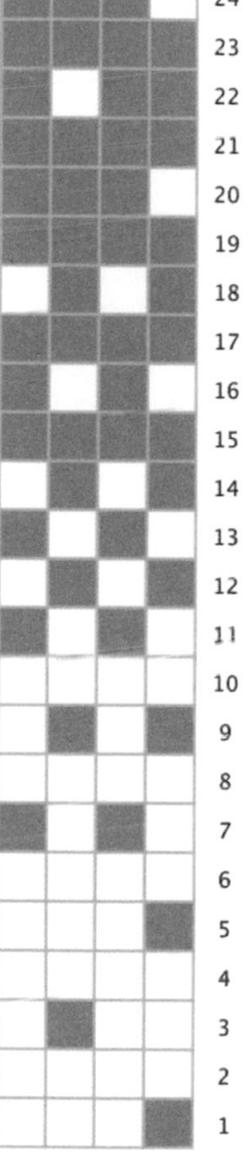

Pattern notes

Be careful to read ahead before jumping in – the afterthought thumb is worked at the same time as the colourwork, and you don't want to miss it!

Pattern

With A, cast on 44 (52, 56, 60) sts. Join to work in the rnd, being careful not to twist.pm to indicate start of rnd. Work in twisted rib for approximately 3 cm.
Begin working in St st with A until mitt is approximately 5 (6, 6.5, 7) cm from cast on edge. Add in B and begin working colourwork transition from chart or written instructions.
After finishing Rnd 24, drop A and work in St st with B for approximately 2 (2.5, 3, 4) cm.
Work colourwork transition with B and C. After finishing Rnd 24, drop B and work in St st with C until mitt is approximately 21 (23, 25, 27)cm long from cast on edge, or approximately 2.5 cm shorter than desired length. Work in twisted rib for 1.5 cm. Cast off loosely.
AT THE SAME TIME, when mitt is approximately 15 (16.5, 17, 19) cm long (or desired length to base of thumb), work afterthought thumb as follows:

Right hand:

At the start of the next rnd, and using waste yarn, k7. Return 7 sts to left needle, drop waste yarn, and work 7 waste yarn sts in pattern with the appropriate colours. Continue working in pattern to end of rnd.

Left hand:

Work to the last 7 sts in pattern. With waste yarn, k7. Return 7 sts to left needle, drop waste yarn, and work 7 waste yarn sts in pattern with the appropriate colours.

Continue working in pattern as described above.

Finishing

Return to thumb and carefully pick out waste yarn, placing 14 live sts on to 2 DPNs. Using a 3.5 mm crochet hook and either A or C, use single crochet to cast off the live sts around the thumb hole. Weave in ends, and block to measurements.

ZIGGING HAT AND COWL

By Renée Callahan

It's no secret that the UK can be a bit chilly in the winter. Or in the summer, as the temperamental British weather can sometimes forget that July and August are supposed to be warm and sunny.If you're visiting London and the temperature turns cooler, this hat and cowl are the perfect antidote. Worked up in a gorgeous, hand dyed Aran weight yarn, both pieces can be made with less than 350 m of yarn. With striking geometric lace and an easy-to-work stitch pattern, this pair would make a great gift for men or women.

Materials:

Kettle Yarn Co. Waltham, 2 skeins in Falconbrook
Aran weight; 166 m per 100 g skein; 100% British Bluefaced Leicester wool

Needles
5.5 mm circular needle, 60 cm, or DPNs

Gauge
15 sts x 22.5 rnds = 10 cm measured over St st

Other supplies
stitch marker

Sizing
Hat: 50 cm circumference, 18.5 cm height
Cowl: 80 cm circumference, 30 cm height

Cable Stitches
C1B: Cable 1 st back without a cable needle by rearranging the 2 sts: Insert RH needle tip into the front of the second st on LH needle, slide both first and second sts off LH needle, and immediately put first st back on to LH needle from behind the second st, then slip the second st from RH needle back onto LH needle, so it is now the first st.
Work sts as usual.

Pattern notes
The beginning of the rnd 'moves' 1 st forward as the pattern spirals around. Mark the first k2tog 'column' rather than space between sts to keep track of the beginning of the rnd.

Hat
With yarn held double, cast on 72 sts. Join to work in the rnd, being careful not to twist. Cut one yarn and continue hat with single strand of yarn.pm to mark beg of rnd (see Pattern Notes above).
Rnds 1-8: *K2, p4; rep from * to end.
Rnds 9-13: *K2tog, yo, k10; rep from * to last 12 sts, k2tog, yo, k9.
Rnd 14: Purl.
Rnds 15-26: *Yo, ssk, k10; rep from * to last 12 sts, yo, ssk, k9.

Crown decreases
Rnd 27 (dec rnd): *Yo, sssk, k9; rep from * to last 12 sts, yo, sssk, k8 - 66 sts.
Rnd 28: *Yo, ssk, k9; rep from * to last 11 sts, yo, ssk, k8.
Rep the last 2 rows 5 more times - 36 sts.
Rep the dec rnd 3 more times - 18 sts.

Break yarn and thread through rem sts.
Pull tight to fasten.

Finishing
Weave in ends and block to dimensions given.

Cowl

Cast on 120 sts. Join to work in the rnd, being careful not to twist.pm to mark beg of rnd (see Pattern Notes above).
Rnd 1-7: *K2, p4; rep from * to end.
Rnds 8-12: *K2tog, yo, k10; rep from * to last 12 sts, k2tog, yo, k9.
Rnd 13: Purl.
Rnds 14-56: *Yo, ssk, k10; rep from * to last 12 sts, yo, ssk, k9.
Rnd 57: Purl.
Rnd 58-62: *K2tog, yo, k10; rep from * to last 12 sts, k2tog, yo, k9.
Rnd 63: *C1B, p4, k2, p4; rep from * to end.
Rnd 64-69: *K2, p4; rep from * to end.
Cast off.

Finishing

Weave in ends and block to dimensions given.

MINI CRAFT CRAWLS

How do you organise your own craft crawl? These types of crawls originally started in knitting communities in North America, usually in cities where there were a variety of shops to choose from. Think of a yarn crawl as the knitter's version of a pub crawl – it's an opportunity to visit a number of shops, each with different offerings, and to experience what makes each shop special.

Yarn crawls are a great way to bring the knitting community together and make new friends. But you don't have to wait until there's one in your town to participate, and we've made a list of a few below to get you started on your way in London.

Some tips for organising your crawl:
1. Figure out which shops are in your local area and/or are easy to get to via public transport.

We use Google as well as Knitmap for yarn shops (www.knitmap.com) to get a sense of the shops in the area and where exactly they're located. Of course, now that you've got the London Craft Guide, you've got plenty to choose from!

2. Decide whether you'll be using public transport or driving or cycling on your craft crawl, as it may make a difference in how many shops you can include.

In London, we definitely recommend public transport, as driving can be slower then anything else, including walking in some cases.

3. Once you know what shops you'd like to visit, plot your route. Our yarn crawls typically finish with some kind of party, so you might want to end up in a pub or café to cast on a new purchase, or admire what your friends have bought and have a piece of cake. If you know where you want to finish, start with the shop the farthest away from that point.

Depending on how many shops you're visiting, you'll also want to pace yourself. Think about how much time you'll want to spend in each shop, how much time you'll need to get to the next one, and when the shops are open. This might mean you can only visit one to two shops in the morning before needing a break for lunch, so plan accordingly.

4. Do your research. Check out the websites for each of the shops that you plan to visit. What do they offer that's of interest and different from the other shops you'll be visiting? Make a list of anything specific you'd like to see. If you're shopping for a particular project, make sure you note yarn weight and yardage quantities that you'll need, as well as any notions or needle sizes.

5. Think about your footwear! Comfy shoes are a must if there will be any significant walking on your crawl. Factor in time for a break for lunch or snacks as needed. It's also a good idea to carry a bottle of water and some extra munchies, in case you need a pick-me-up along the way.

The mini crawls suggested are organised largely by geography, and ease of transfer between the shops. We've also tried to include a range of shops, so you're not seeing the same thing at each stopping point. Don't let these recommendations limit you – take a look at the georgraphical groupings in the rest of the book and let your imagination run wild!

Transportation

Getting around London can be a challenge, depending on the time of year, the time of day and the ever-changing weather! Here are some of our favourite online resources to make your journey as easy as possible:

Apps

Citymapper
(web version at citymapper.com)

Websites

Transport for London
(particularly their Journey Planner)
tfl.gov.uk

National Rail
nationalrail.co.uk

Central:
John Lewis – Liberty – V V Rouleaux – Berwick Street

The Village Haberdashery – I Knit – Patricia Roberts

North:
Nest – Handweavers Studio & Gallery – Loop

Loop – I Knit – The Village Haberdashery

East:
Fabrications – Wild & Woolly – Knit with Attitude

Knit with Attitude – Fringe – Wild & Woolly

Stitch Glossary

B	place bead and knit
Beg	begin(ning)
CC	contrast colour
Ch	chain
Ch-sp	chain space
Dc	double crochet
Dec	decrease(d)
Garter st	Garter stitch
Inc	increase(d)
K	knit
K2tog	knit two together: 1 st dec.
M1	make a backwards loop and place it on the right needle - 1 st inc.
M1R	insert left needle, from back to front, under the horizontal strand that lies between the st just knit, and the following st; knit into the front of this loop - 1 st inc.
M1L	insert left needle, from front to back, under the horizontal strand that lies between the st just knit, and the following st; knit into the back of this loop - 1 st inc.
MC	main colour
P	purl
Pm	place marker
P2tog	purl two sts together
Rep	repeat
Rnd	round
RS	right side of work
Sk2p	slip one st as if to knit, k2tog, pass slipped st over – 2 sts dec.
Sl	slip
Sm	slip marker
Ss	slip st
Ssk	slip, slip, knit: slip two sts one at a time as if to knit, insert the left needle through the front of the slipped sts and knit them together through the back loop – 1 st dec.
St st	stocking st
St(s)	stitch(es)
Tbl	through the back loop
Tr	treble crochet
WS	wrong side of work
W&t	wrap and turn: Slip next st onto the right needle purlwise. Move the yarn to the other side of the work, and slip the unworked st back to the left hand needle. Move the yarn back to the other side of the work, wrapping the st. Turn the work. To pick up wraps: Use the tip of the right needle to pick up the wrap(s) from front to back if on RS, or from back to front if on WS. Work the st and wrap(s) together.
Yo	yarn over

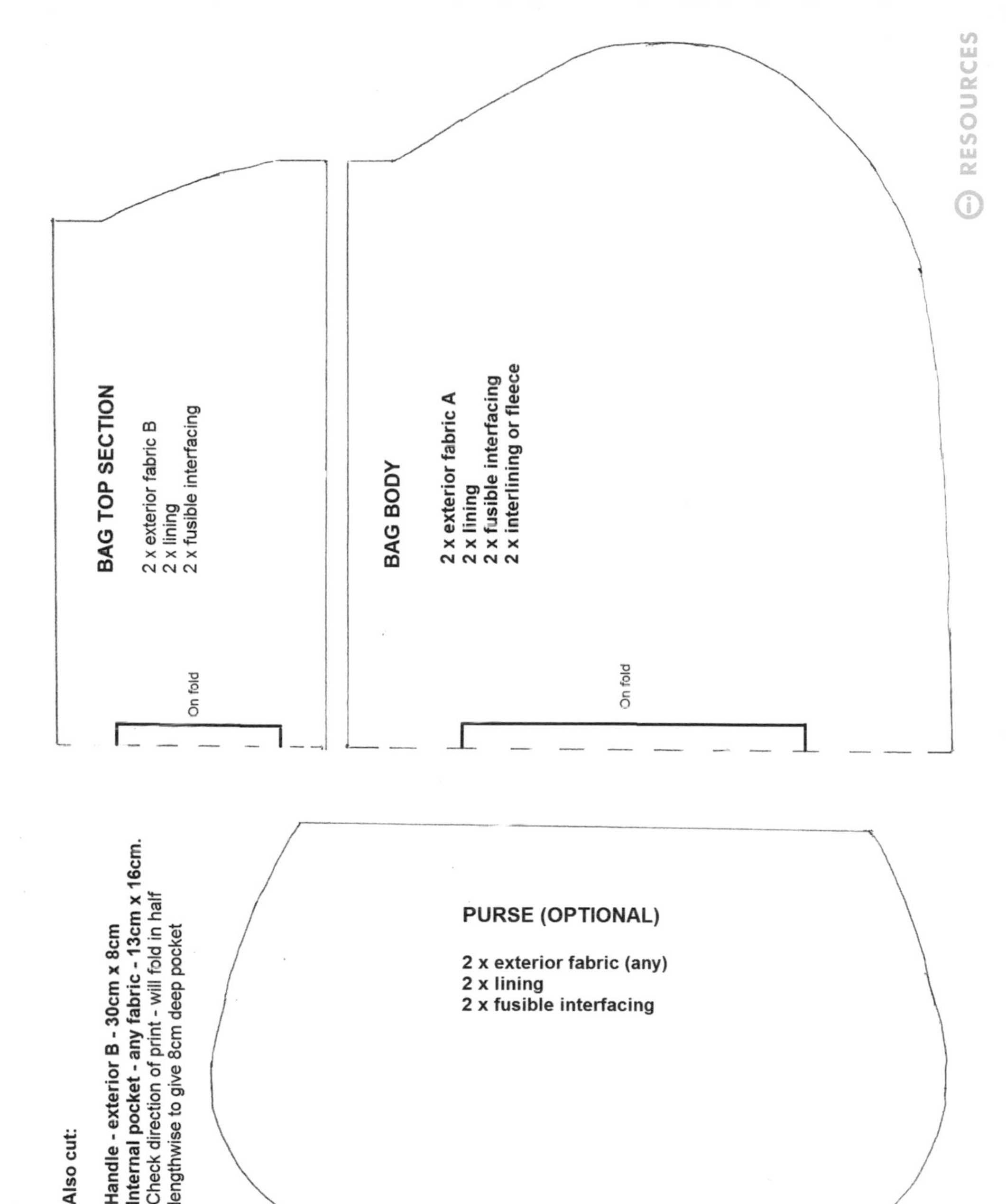

Going Underground Bag Pattern pieces

Copy page, adjusting size to 100% scale on borderless A4. The width of the small purse at the widest point should be16.5 cm.

YARN IN THE CITY

Rachel and Allison are North American expats who enjoy living in London and being part of the UK knitting community.

Founded in early 2013, Yarn in the City celebrates the yarn-loving community of knitters and fibre enthusiasts in London and the UK by creating experiential yarn-centric events designed to bring people together in a shared love of craft. Yarn in the City also hosts a weekly knit night in SW London and records a podcast featuring chat about the goings-on in the UK yarn and fibre community, books and yarn reviews and interviews with special guests.

The Great London Yarn Crawl – a one-day tour of London's finest yarn and haberdashery shops - is Yarn in the City's annual charity event. Since 2013 the event has raised over £2,500 for UK charity Refuge, providing support to victims of domestic violence.

Rachel Brown

Rachel is a knitwear designer and tech-editor-for-hire. She has been published in Knit Now, Knitty and KnittySpin as well as self-publishing her designs on Ravelry. Rachel is also the colour-mad scientist behind Porpoise Fur (porpoisefur.com), purveyor of gorgeous, hand-dyed fibres for your spinning pleasure. Porpoise Fur fibres have been featured in KnittySpin and in the Phat Fiber and Spinning Box sampler boxes.

Allison Thistlewood

Allison is the UK sales rep for SweetGeorgia Yarns and The Fibre Co. Allison is also a marketing and communications professional specialising in digital and social media. Her clients span the spectrum of the yarn and fibre industry from designers to indie dyers and local shops. You can find Allison blogging about her knitting adventures at Champagne & Qiviut (champagneandqiviut.com).